THE MARKAS

an anthology of literary works on
Boko Haram

THE MARKAS

an anthology of literary works on
Boko Haram

Edited by

Tanure Ojaide   Razinat Mohammed
Abubakar Othman   Hyeladzira Balami

malthouse 𝄞𝒫

Malthouse Press Limited

Lagos, Benin, Ibadan, Jos, Port-Harcourt, Zaria

Published and manufactured in Nigeria by

Malthouse Press Limited
43 Onitana Street, Off Stadium Hotel Road,
Off Western Avenue, Lagos Mainland
E-mail: malthouselagos@gmail.com
Tel: +234 802 600 3203

Distributors:

African Books Collective Ltd
Email: abc@africanbookscollective.com
Website: http://www.africanbookscollective.com

To

All whose lives in one way or another have been affected by
Boko Haram

Editors' Note

This anthology is a collection of literary responses to the Boko Haram insurgency in the north-eastern part of Nigeria. As the Introduction explains, the socio-cultural, economic, and political lives of the people have all been negatively impacted by the fundamentalist organization's violent tactics that have resulted in not only deaths but dislocation of millions of people in the affected areas. Those who knew the area before 2009 know the high level of dislocation and destruction which have taken place. Most people have taken refuge in urban centres like Maiduguri for safety. Many refugees are in Internally Displaced Persons' camps guarded by Nigerian soldiers.

Writers in the affected areas and other parts of Nigeria where there are constant news reports of Boko Haram have responded in the forms of poetry, short stories, and non-fiction which are assembled here to tell their thoughts and feelings about Boko Haram, a highly dreaded group. It will be seen how different writers respond to the Boko Haram experience. The Introduction summarizes the background to the insurgency for readers to fully understand the nature of responses in the literary mode.

We believe that however long it may take, peace will be restored in the north-eastern part of Nigeria. It is with that hope that we want to record the lived experiences of people at this particular period of Nigerian history. We also hope that a future edition of this anthology will include some of the experiences and literary responses which are not available to us at this time.

Editors

Ojaide, Tanure - A Fellow in Writing of the University of Iowa, Tanure Ojaide was educated at the University of Ibadan, where he received a bachelor's degree in English, and at Syracuse University, where he received both M.A. in Creative Writing and Ph.D. in English. His literary awards include the Commonwealth Poetry Prize for the Africa Region (1987), the All-Africa Okigbo Prize for Poetry (1988, 1997), the BBC Arts and Africa Poetry Award (1988), and the Association of Nigerian Authors Poetry Award (1988, 1994, 2003, and 2011). In 2016 he won both the African Literature Association's Folon-Nichols Award for Excellence in Writing and the Nigerian National Order of Merit Award for the Humanities. Ojaide taught for many years at The University of Maiduguri (Nigeria), and is currently The Frank Porter Graham Professor of Africana Studies at The University of North Carolina at Charlotte.

Mohammed, Razinat T. - An Associate Professor of Feminist Literary Criticism at the University of Maiduguri, she is the award-winning author of *A love Like a Woman's and other Stories*. Her first novel, *Habiba*, was a finalist for the ANA prize for prose 2014; she is also the author of *The Travails of a first Wife* (2015), *Intra-gender Relations between Women: A Study of Nawal El-Saadawi and Buchi Emecheta's Novel* (Germany) and *Female Representation in Nigerian Literature* www.africanwriter.com among others.

Othman, Abubakar A.- He holds a PhD in Literary Psychoanalysis and teaches African poetry and Creative Writing at the University of Maiduguri. His published works include The Palm of Time (2000, Malthouse), The Passions of Cupid (2013 Kraftbooks), and Blood Streams in the Desert (2013 Kraftbooks)

Balami, Hyeladzira – Hyeladzira is a lecturer in the Department of English and Literary Studies, University of Maiduguri. He has a forthcoming book of poetry.

Contributors

Abubakar, Mujtaba S. – He is a Nigerian creative writer.

Agema, Su'ur Eddie Vershima – He is an editor, an award-winning author and development worker. He has four poetry collections, a children's book and a short story collection. He blogs at http://sueddie.wordpress.com.

Agoi, Folu – President of PEN International, Nigerian Centre, erstwhile Chairman, Association of Nigerian Authors Lagos, multiple award winning writer–he is a creative writer, poet, critic, literary activist, editor, publisher and teacher.

Amajuoyi, Olive Chinyere – She is a writer whose major focus is poetry and fiction. She has written over 100 articles and essays either published on her website: idealolive.blogspot.com or presented as a speech. She lives and works in Enugu, Nigeria.

Bariki, Ruth - has just completed her Master's program in the Department of English at the University of Lagos.

Chukwu, George – He is a freelance writer. He has written articles for blogs and websites in different niches but mainly on personal development. He has written over 200 articles for his clients and fellow writers. He is working on his novel and lives at Ojota, Lagos State.

Eke, Iquo Diana Abasi – Iquo writes prose, poetry and scripts for radio and screen. Her first collection of poems was shortlisted for the NLNG Nigeria prize for literature, and the ANA poetry prize; both in 2013.It was also shortlisted for the Wole Soyinka Literature Prize, 2018. She lives in Lagos.

El-Mubashir, Abdulsalam – He is a Nigerian creative writer.

Giwa, Audee T. - An Associate Professor of English with Kaduna State University in Nigeria. Born in 1961, he is the author of four novels - *I'd rather Die, Marks on the Run, From Fatika with Love, Yarinya* - and two short story collections, *Love in the afternoon* and *Ancestral Wrath.*

Giwewhegbe, Uvie - Uvie has a Master's degree from the Department of English at the University of Lagos. She writes plays and poetry and is the author of *The Man With The White Hat,* a collection of short stories published by Malthouse (2018).

Idrisu, Adama H. – He is a Chief Lecturer at Mohammed Goni College of Legal and Islamic Studies Maiduguri. He has published poems in International Poets and World Poetry.

Imam, Khalid – He is a poet and multiple awards–winning bilingual playwright. He is the Vice Chairman of Association of Nigerian Authors Kano State branch and a Board of Trustee Member of Poets In Nigeria.

Jacob, Anita – is from Abia State, Nigeria. She is a final year student at the Department of English and Literary Studies, Niger Delta University, Amassoma, Bayelsa State. She is a blogger.

Joda, Abubakar M. - Joda is a student of pharmacy at Gombe State University, Gombe State. He has a passion for short fiction and poetry.

Kaase, Rachel Msendoo – She is a Nigerian creative writer.

Maina, Hassana U. Hassana Umoru Maina is from Borno State, Nigeria. She is a law student at the Ahmadu Bello University, Zaria. She is the current Chairperson of the Creative Writers Club, ABU Zaria. She is presently working on her first novel.

Mustafa, Linda Jummai – She currently teaches at Ibrahim Badamasi Babangida University, Lapai, Niger State.

Ogechi, Ofoko - Ofoko is a Nigerian creative writer.

Okpanachi, Idris Musa – He is an award-winning poet who has published in reputable international journals like *Presence*

Africaine (Paris), Kunapipi (Denmark), Pyramids, Iraq Literary Review, and *Ufaham: Journal of African Studies* in the United States. He teaches at Federal University, Dutse.

Olaifa, Mojolaoluwa - Mojolaoluwa Olaifa is a Lawyer, Writer and an Activist. In 2018, she was a finalist in the 2018 Africa Book Club Sort Story Competition. Mojolaoluwa is also an Associate Fellow of the Royal Commonwealth Society, a network of individuals and organisations committed to improving the lives and prospects of Commonwealth citizens across the world through youth empowerment, education and advocacy. Mojolaoluwa is the Team Lead, Leaders of Today Nigeria, an initiative dedicated to creating the largest network of credible and sound minds that are constantly giving their best to the growth of the nation in ways they can and giving them the right exposure nationally and globally.

Salawu, Tolani - Tolani Salawu is a Marriage Counsellor, an inspirational writer, a philanthropist and advocate of Good Life for the Girl Child and a member of Association of Nigerian Authors. Tolani has written over one hundred articles on attitudes and lifestyles.

Sylvester, Vicky – She is a Professor of Literature and Gender Studies in the Department of English and Literary Studies, University of Abuja, Abuja FCT

Vincent, Jack – He was born and raised in Maiduguri, northeast of Nigeria. He is a trained journalist with specialty in humanitarian access and negotiations. He is the current Secretary of the Association of Nigerian Authors (ANA), Borno State Chapter.

Yerima, Adama Balla - was born on December 19, 1974 in Maiduguri, Borno State. She was afflicted by polio as an infant and suffers severe disabilities. Despite her physical challenges, she has authored two books, a collection of poetry and a play. She is the founder of Zadaya-Kanen Polio Disabilities Initiative and now works as social mobilization officer of the National Primary Health Care Development Agency (NPHCDA). She is married and lives in Maiduguri.

Yerima, Nereus Tadi - He is a lecturer at the Department of English, Gombe State University. He has published two poetry collections and three texts on Tangle Studies.

Yero, Safiya Ismail – She is a poet and author of *When There is Life* and *Naja*, a full-length novel to be published by Malthouse in May 2019. She currently works at the University of Abuja.

Yohanna, Daniel - hails from Cham district, Balanga L.G.A of Gombe State Nigeria. He has a flair for poetry and novels. His stage name is Nature.

Zugu, Benjamin Armstrong – He hails from Guma local government in Benue state, and is currently a final year student of English and Literary Studies, University of Maiduguri.

Contents

PART II   THE DIALOGUE POEMS

PART III   FICTION AND NON-FICTION

Introduction

The Boko Haram Phenomenon: challenges for the Nigerian State and Society

- Tanure Ojaide

Boko Haram is often seen in the same global and transnational context of Islamic fundamentalism as *Al Qaeda*; *Al Qaeda* in the Islamic Maghreb, Islamic State/ISIS, Taliban, and *Al Shabaab* in the Horn of Africa. These are radical Islamist movements that gained inspiration from Osama bin Laden. There is no doubt that the Western/NATO-assisted overthrow of Muammar Gadhafi has unleashed terrorists from the routed army and members of the Islamic State in the Maghreb to migrate southwards to Mali and Nigeria in particular. One can say that Boko Haram is a local phenomenon based in northern Nigeria but is part of what could be described as a franchise of the transnational Islamist movement and with global ramifications. Elements of Boko Haram also operate in adjacent territories of Cameroon, Chad, and Niger.

"Boko Haram" in Hausa means "Western education is a sin." The real name of this Islamic sect is *Jama'atu Ahlus Sunnah Lidda'awati wal-Jihad*, which means People Committed to the Prophet's Teachings and Jihad. The members of the sect prefer to be called *Yusufiyya* sect after their founding leader,

Mohammed Yusuf, killed under mysterious circumstances while in police custody in Maiduguri in 2009. Boko Haram adherents are fundamentalist Muslims concerned about Western thoughts, lifestyle, dress, and politics and their perceived negative impact on the Nigerian society. In 2002 Yusuf built a school and a mosque to inculcate Islamic religious values on young Muslims in Maiduguri. The sect thus started as a traditional Qur'anic Islamic school, tagging Western education a "sin". The sect was thus relatively unknown until the death of its founder. Henceforth, under the leadership of Abubakar Shekau, the sect escalated its violence that has affected the safety and security of Nigerians, especially in the north-eastern part of the country.

The infrastructures that started Boko Haram were established in 2002. However, a school of thought attributes two parallel movements that coalesced into the Boko Haram of today: the "ECOMOG" of Borno State Governor, Ali Modu Sheriff, for eight years and the militarization of Borno State and the arrest and perceived judicial killing of the group's leader, Mohammed Yusuf. Ali Modu Sheriff recruited body guards nicknamed "ECOMOG," after the West African Peace-Keeping troops in Liberia and later Sierra Leone. Starting at about a dozen, the guards grew to about eight truckloads half of which were in front and the other half behind in Sheriff's motorcade. He lavished money on them from his huge security vote. After his governorship, the unemployed bodyguards became disgruntled and sought to overthrow the Borno State Government by seizing police stations. The group became a rallying point for disgruntled unemployed Kanuri elements, hence their presence in Borno, Yobe, and the northern part of Adamawa States. Following the disclosure by the Australian mediator between the Nigerian Government and Boko Haram that Sheriff funded Boko Haram; the former governor has in forceful terms in Abuja denied any relationship with the Islamist group.

The other narrative of the beginning of Boko Haram as a violent group begins from 2009. The high military and security presence with their high-handed tactics in Borno State and the arrest and death of Yusuf in police custody are the other reasons. What the group felt they could not do with their school and mosque, they had to do underground through fighting.

Socio-economic inequality resulting in a divided society of haves and have-nots is a major cause of disaffection in the north-eastern area as in many other parts of Nigeria. In these areas the state was expected to provide employment and social amenities to ameliorate the plight of the poor but there was none of this in the country's north-eastern region. There was (and still is) the perception of the poor that the government favours politicians and the rich. Increasingly the poor feel marginalized and neglected. The disaffection caused by poverty also makes the poor not cooperate with security forces in combating violence or terrorism. Poverty of youths thus creates the enabling environment for mobilization and recruitment for terrorist activities.

Islam favours Qur'anic schools and promotes alms-giving and thus making *almajiris* beholden to their *malams* and rich Muslims. Young pupils are often taught about the possibilities of martyrdom, which makes the young ones not care about giving up their lives to kill in the name of Islam. Another factor that is often ignored is the distaste of some Muslims for the corruption of the Nigerian state and society. This corruption fuels the fanaticism of those who prefer an austere clean life. Fighting the infidels who are corrupt becomes an appealing slogan.

Shehu Sani has listed the following as the causes of Boko Haram:

1. Repressive attack against the religious group by the Government in 2009;
2. The extra judicial killings of their Leader Muhammad Yusuf and others in 2009;
3. Exclusion of members of the Group by mainstream Islamic groups;
4. Failure of Governance in Borno and Bauchi states;
5. Federal government policy of appeasing militancy;
6. Inspiration from the success of the armed struggle in the Niger Delta;
7. Abject poverty and high rate of unemployment in the northern states;
8. Proliferation of arms in the north east;
9. Chadian civil war and illegal immigration;
10. Disconnect between elected and appointed leaders and the people;
11. Absence of data and intelligence about individuals and organizational links with foreign groups;
12. Absence of a rehabilitation program for religious fundamentalists;
13. Indolence and negligence of the northern states governors;
14. Misuse of security votes by state Governors;
15. The standoff in Somalia;
16. Unresolved Arab-Israeli crisis;
17. Lack of true federalism;

18. Resistance of the political establishment to a national conference;
19. The collapse of public schools;
20. Active involvement of traditional leaders in politics; and
21. Federal government's increasing reliance on foreign security agencies.

Boko Haram has unleashed a reign of terror across the north-eastern and other parts of Nigeria. Boko Haram's terrorism has involved killing/slaughter of innocent folks and in their homes, roads, and schools; suicide bombing of UN Office in Abuja; churches; mosques; markets; supermarkets; Nyanya bus station; and other public places. They have kidnapped many girls and women as from Chibok and raped them, and also kidnapped young boys and girls to recruit for suicide bombing and their army.

It has challenged the Nigerian Government to react on how best to make the citizens safe and provide security nationwide. There is loss of lives and the kidnapping of the Chibok girls and other women has exposed the Government's weakness. In fact, Nigeria is being branded a failed state because of the helplessness of the security apparatus in dealing with Boko Haram. The Government has struggled to react to the phenomenon in many ways, some of which have made things worse.

The Federal Government seems to intensify the militarization by sending troops that are incompetent in fighting the insurgents in addition to the use of obsolete war machineries. The arrest and killing of Mohammed Yusuf in 2009 inflamed the insurgency. Boko Haram has ironically become far better armed and motivated than the State it is fighting. Nigerian Army troops tend to retreat with the advance of the terrorist group.

The Nigerian Government initiated a Presidential Committee to investigate the security challenges in the north-eastern part of Nigeria, especially Borno State. The Committee summarized their findings as the killing of Mohammed Yusuf, founder of the sect; militarization of the area; and the hard approach of security personnel as responsible for the terrorism. Other ways the Government has reacted to Boko Haram include:

1. In 2011, the FG enacted the anti-terrorism act declaring Boko Haram a terrorist group.
2. The Security Conference organized by CLEEN, an NGO based in Abuja, where Abubakar Mua'zu and many with military and security expertise spoke on strategies to curtail the excesses of Boko Haram.
3. The Federal Government declared a state of emergency in Borno, Yobe, and Adamawa States in 2013. The state of emergency further militarized the areas of operation of Boko Haram.
4. On April 14, 2014 Boko Haram kidnapped 276 Chibok Girls from their secondary school hostels at night. The Federal Government's response to protesters drawing attention to their plight has been to malign and badly treat them such as the temporary "detention" of Dr. Oby Ezekwesili, perhaps the best known of the protesters in Abuja. This shows that the protesters on the ground in Abuja face the ire of the Federal Government, unlike those who join the protest on the Internet or from abroad who are free and fall silent once the subject is no longer current.

5. The Federal Government initiated a Presidential Committee to investigate the circumstances surrounding the kidnapping of the Chibok girls. It was over 100days after the incident and after the visit of the Pakistani girl and education activist Malala's visit that President Jonathan even met the escaped girls and the parents of the kidnapped school girls. There is thus the perception of a rudderless government incapable of providing safety and security for its citizens.

6. Nigeria's Council of State met at the Presidential Villa, Abuja, on Thursday, August 1, 2014 to discuss the insurgency of Boko Haram and pledging to end it by December 2014 through a series of measures.

7. The Federal Government is held accountable and perceived as the only one through its army that can stop the insurrection. A group of the Northern Elders Forum led by Maitama Sule gave President Jonathan an ultimatum to get the Chibok girls free by December or not run for the Presidency in the February 2015 Elections. At the same time Members of the Nigerian Army Officers' Wives Association appealed to the President not to send their husbands to fight Boko Haram because the Nigerian Army is poorly armed against a well-armed terrorist group.

8. The rampant corruption in the entire Nigerian system (Army and Government), poor governance, and the disorganized, inadequate, and low moral nature of the security forces have led to the boldness of the terrorist group and the loss of land to it.

9. The porous borders of Nigeria and neighbouring states may be allowing foreign fighters to join Boko Haram and reinforce the arms seized from retreating Nigerian Army.

10. Boko Haram may not be as rich as ISIS but it is modestly rich. There are suspicions of very important Nigerians contributing to their coffers and the Central Bank of Nigeria has been accused of being a financial conduit to the sect.

The on-going phenomenon of terrorism has caused lack of safety and security in the affected areas. It has caused massive displacement of people. One estimate by the National Commission for Refugees is that 600,000 people have been displaced because of the violent conflict in the Northeast (August 19, 2014).

The consequences of the Boko Haram terrorism are far-reaching. The insurrection has caused disruption of socio-economic life in the areas. The insurgency has disrupted commerce, education, youth development, and other aspects of life in the affected areas. For instance, there used to be many traders bringing foodstuffs from the South and buying fish from Baga to sell in the Southeast. That trade has virtually halted. The attacks on markets in Maiduguri and other towns as well as shopping malls in Abuja and Kano have made it difficult for folks to shop in such places.

One of the core issues Boko Haram is fighting is Western education, which they believe encourages immoral lifestyles. That has made them to focus attacks on Western style schools. After attacks on schools in Yobe, Borno, and other affected areas, elementary and secondary schools in particular closed. Thus children and youths are denied education which should be their key to progress in life. With the example of the slaughter of students in boarding schools as the Federal Government College in Bunu Yadi, Yobe State, and others and the mass abduction of girls in Chibok, there is fear of attending school. The northeast parts of Nigeria that were not developed before the insurrection have been further set backward, compared to the Southern states of the country that have not been touched by the Islamic terrorism.

Other aspects of life affecting individual safety and security for all appear to have arrested development in the Boko Haram-affected areas. Ironically, without schools and commerce, the poverty rate will intensify and doom the current generation of young ones.

It is the boys, girls, and young ones that are the greatest losers in the Boko Haram phenomenon in the Northeast and other parts of Northern Nigeria. The unemployed and poor youths are recruited into the group to fight the State. Many of these youths who do not see a future for themselves in the Nigerian state are further brainwashed and promised martyrdom and its heavenly life of bliss to fight the morally corrupt government at state and federal levels. These mobilized and recruited youths become perpetrators of terror and violence destroying the society and weakening the state. As earlier stated, these youths are more like anarchists in the manner in which they kill by bombing churches, mosques, markets, malls, kidnapping, and unleashing other forms of violence on the society.

Ironically, youths and women are the main victims of the Boko Haram insurgency. Young ones are arrested and sometimes killed as supporters of the sect. Women are especially vulnerable in their being kidnapped. The example of the kidnapped Chibok girls and other women from the same area is very instructive about the vulnerability of women.

It must be noted that the youth agency is not always negative. Youths in some areas such as Maiduguri have formed vigilante groups that guard their neighbourhoods from being attacked by Boko Haram. In fact, since they are familiar with their neighbourhoods and know many members of the Boko Haram, they seem to be doing a better job about safeguarding people more than the military. My angst is that the youths who are supposed to be the inheritors in society are being damaged physically and psychologically and put out of school and self-development. The earlier the Islamist insurrection ends, the better for the youths and the rest of society.

The following listed possible solutions are summaries of what security experts, politicians, journalists, and scholars have recommended.

- There is growing consensus that to defeat Boko Haram that its ideology has to be addressed through a political process.
- The Federal Government should not pursue only a military option since that will make it more difficult to solve the problem because past experience has shown that harsh military tactics alienate the people from the Government. In addition, Boko Haram seems to be better armed than the corrupt and inefficient Nigerian Army whose soldiers flee at the approach of Boko Haram as happened in Damboa and other garrison towns. A military solution is also difficult as many officers of the Nigerian Army are Muslim and some, if not many, senior officers sympathize with and assist Boko Haram. In 2013 the soldiers sent to combat Boko Haram mutinied against the GOC who was investigated and found cooperating with the insurgents and was removed.
- Empowering youths to shrink the pool from which Boko Haram recruits its fighters. Ironically, this will involve

sending the youths, boys and girls, to school to get good education and then good jobs that will make them less willing to join a terrorist group. This also involves economic empowerment with the creation of jobs to make them positively occupied and resistant to political and religious manipulation. In addition to employment, others that cannot be employed should be given cash and the opportunity to do something else than suicide bombing or fighting for Boko Haram.

- There should be a political side to solving the Boko Haram problem. This should aim at making Northern political and traditional leaders to assume a stronger role in stopping the carnage and the developmental arrest in their areas. These leaders should dissociate themselves from the extremist Islamists. There is the prevalent view that some Northern politicians were privy to the activities of Boko Haram which were explained in jihadist and political terms in the context of the Nigerian state. There is the feeling among many Nigerians that Muhammadu Buhari, a chieftain of the APC while in the CPC was through his statements supporting the terrorist group. However, it appears things escalated and Northern politicians saw that the pet has turned into a monster!

- The Federal and State Governments should fight to reduce corruption that grows poverty of the common people and youths and is a moral outrage to pious people that want to fight it.

- I recommend the establishment of a Peace Fund for conscious and special development of the Northeast and other parts of Northern Nigeria to bring them to a level as many of the Southern States. This sacrifice is meant to ensure peace in the country because uneven development leads to disaffection and violence in the form of terrorism.

- There should be amnesty for members of the sect who surrender and renounce terrorism. Such members should be assisted in vocations as done for the ex-militants from the Niger Delta region.
- The media should be used to campaign for peace. There should be development and broadcast of security tips in the mass media. These organs should enlighten the public on the role of the people in deterring and disrupting terrorist attacks.
- Installing CCTV cameras in strategic places such as plazas, malls, crowded places, churches, and mosques. Monitoring the cameras will help prevent some terrorist acts and also facilitate the solving of suicide bombings.
- There should be intelligence and information sharing among Nigeria, Cameroon, Chad, and Nigeria, a process which has started.
- Bring Islamic leaders from countries like Senegal and Malaysia for a conference or workshop on Islam in diverse and multi-ethnic states. Nigerian Muslims in the extreme North will learn from others what makes them to live peacefully with others.

It is incumbent on the Federal Government to pursue a multifarious approach towards resolving the problem to bring much needed peace to the area and with peace, safety, and security, the society will thrive on education, commerce, and general development. Also with peace, the state will be seen as protecting the interests of its citizens and fulfilling its role as an effective government.

References and Works Cited

Bartollota, C. "Terrorism in Nigeria: The Rise of Boko Haram," *The Whitehead Journal of Diplomacy and International Relations*, www.blogs.shu.edu/diplomacy/2011/09/terrorism-in nigeria.

FRGN (Federal Republic of Nigeria). The Prevention of Terrorism Act 2011.

Ibaba, Samuel Ibaba. "The Roots of Terrorism in Nigeria: Exploring the Poverty Connection." *Africana Journal*, vol. 6, no. 2 (March 2013), 188-217.

---. "Violent Conflicts and sustainable Development in Bayelsa State." *Review of African Political Economy*, No. 122 (2009), 555-573.

Mu'azu, Abubakar. "Understanding the Emerging Trends of Terrorism in Nigeria: A Case Study of Boko Haram and Similar Groups." Conference Proceedings, *Responding to the Emerging Trends of Terrorism in Nigeria*, CLEEN Foundation Nigeria, Monograph Series No 16 (2011), 10-21.

Sani, Shehu. 'Causes of Boko Haram' Nigeria's Boko Haram: The Way Forward, <http://shelusam.blogspot.com/2011/06/nigeria-boko-haram--way-forward.html Accessed August 1, 2014).

United Nations. Draft International Convention on International Terrorism. www.un.org/law/terrorism/ (2004).

PART I

POETRY

NEREUS TADI YERIMA[*]

Sister, the sky is grey again

Sister, the sky is grey again
Grey again, grey again
Ah, sister, sister, the times
The times play foul
We have fallen into thorns
Into dry piercing thorns
We count our loses
Loses in the past year
Our husbands gone
Our children maimed
Our houses, our houses destroyed
Living in make-shift tents
Like herdsmen and their seasons
Ah, sister, sister, the blisters on our feet
We have seen places strange
We, children of Boko Haram are witnesses
In the strange world of IDPs
Where the giants of NEMA
Flash golden teeth to the dispossessed
We have heard tales
Sweet tales of truckloads of goods
On their way...
Then missing on the way...
Ah, sister, sister
The road, the road is rough

---

[*] **Nereus Yerima Tadi** is a lecturer at the Department of English, Gombe State University. He has published two poetry collections and three texts on Tangle Studies.

Dispersed by Boko Haram
The chaos in Internally Displaced Persons
Ah, IDPs
Neglect of the denuded
Fat cocks feeding on our wounds
I have seen, I have seen the tears
Of children orphaned
Of widows distraught
Despite assurances from the Rock
Despite the news of aids in dollars
I have seen sorrow
Maiden with deadly fangs
Strangle the old
Strangle our babes
In gilded robes
They shout the mercy of gods
To the broken souls
I heard them say…
But sister, sister
It is daybreak
The clouds are gathering
Clear your fields
Sister, clear your fields
Prepare your seedlings
Sister, prepare your seedlings
Let's begin again
The journey to recovery.

News

Flies drive away bees
We are lost
Lost in Sambisa Forest
Our land is lost

Lizards chase away snakes
Our brows are raised
Our hairs erect
We are lost

The pot has broken
The pot has broken
Who can gather it?
Who can mend it?

Ah! We are lost
Lost in the savannah
We are lost
Lost

Prepare to run brother
Sister, on your marks
Women, are you there
Children, it is time to sprint

For we are lost
Lost like rudderless sailors
We are lost
Lost

They say
Gwoza has fallen
Dambua is scattered
Lizards too are scared

We are lost
Lost like MH370
We are lost
Lost

Behold we witnessed
A fearsome dance of vultures
Red dust on the horizon
Blisters on our feet

Brethren
Do you not know?
Bama is feverish
Damaturu wails.

We are lost
Like sheep in the desert
We are lost
Lost

Kano is in heat
Parcels on the hit
Kaduna is in disarray
A girl and a cooler

We are lost
Nightmare in Nyanya
We are lost
Lost

Black banners advance!
Night comes
Like *B*lack *H*ammer
Our night!

Peace will Return

From Chibok wailings rend the air
Peace has gone with the wind
Peace has gone
Peace has gone

Mothers with streamy eyes
Fathers with creased brows
A storm shatters
Elephants on the rampage

And peace is gone
Peace is gone
Birds in a stormy night
Peace is gone

Thrown out of school
Hunger his companion
The orphan cries
For peace denied

In tatters he trudges
With fire-wood shortened neck
Bathed in sweat he smiles
For elusive peace

For peace is gone
Peace is gone
Cripples on a thorny path
Peace is gone

Hyenas and jackals roam the earth
Cobras and puff adders
Venom! Venom!
Dragons swim in pools of blood

In Cairo, a crimson square
Sudan breaks with blows
Libya leaves the lane of love
Ukraine and the cranes of Ibycus

Peace is gone
In the city of peace
Shalom Jerusalem *Sala'am*
And swords are raised!

Rumblings below
Earthquake salutes the world
Rumblings above
Thunder rolls, cracks

I too wail, brother
This bile that churns my insides
I too wail, sister
Splintered bones choke me

Sleep no more!
A murdered bed hisses
Sleep no more
For peace is gone.

Sleep no more
You hearkening ears
Sleep no more
Till peace returns

For peace will return
Gently like the whistling brook
Peace will return
Like the butterfly in floral hours

Queen of the night
Cool and dark
King of the day
Fragrance

Return
O peace return
Return to this famished land
To this charred earth, return.

Peace
Oh peace
We will drink the honey
Despite the stings of bees

Peace
Sweet peace
To you my love
A calabash of milk.

FOLU AGOI*

Tears for Chibok

Nyanya on my mind
And Chibok
Damboa, Gamboru
Gwoza, Guma, Gujba, Baga
Bama, Mubi, Damaturu, Konduga...
Bleeding Hiroshimas, endless list, razed farms raising vultures.

Nyanya on my mind
And Chibok
Leading Hiroshimas starring comic stars
Star comics thrilling crowds, shocking crowds
Toothless daddies dancing disco, cracking jokes, solid jokes
Panting, sweating, striving to spice up their sons' funeral.

Nyanya on my mind
And Chibok
Flaming farms feeding vultures
Starring dandy daddies tending palm wine
Fondling funny mummies singing carols at Requiem Mass
Flaming fools, snail-slow, snake-sly, vulturous like Sambisa.

---

* **Folu Agoi** – President of PEN International, Nigerian Centre, erstwhile Chairman, Association of Nigerian Authors Lagos, multiple award winning writer–he is a creative writer, poet, critic, literary activist, editor, publisher and teacher.

I weep for Nyanya
Chibok, Dikwa, Sanga, Kaga, Kaura...
I weep for Hiroshimas breeding vultures
Bleeding vultures haunting clownish clans
Haunting a town that chose to crown a clown
Grown tortoise bleeding kingdoms, breeding Babylon.

Pray, what manner of father trades his virgin daughters
For a keg of palm wine?

Note
'I was not surprised that the President [Dr Goodluck Jonathan] went dancing [at a political rally in Kano] twenty-four hours after the Nyanya explosion that took seventy-five lives. [The bomb explosion rocked Nyanya Motor Park, on the outskirts of Abuja, on April 14, 2014, killing at least 75 people.] I also found believable the statement allegedly credited to the president after both the Nyanya explosion and the [two hundred and seventy-six, 276] Chibok school girls' abduction to the effect that since some people in the North had said that they would make Nigeria ungovernable, they could keep on killing and abducting each other.' – *Past Nigerian President Olusegun Obasanjo, in his autobiography,* **My Watch (Farafina, 2014)**

Tactical Manoeuvre

Grandpa was a storyteller
Busy bee spinning fables
Honeyed tales tickling toddlers
Like one sour story trailing one gallant soldier
Fabled giant slaying legions, strangling squadrons
Goliath, nay, Samson squashing skulls using fingers;
But one day, facing soldier ants chilling in a ditch
He dumped his name and jumped the fence
Taking refuge under a neighbour's undies
Panting, giant soldier panting
Cringing like a distressed chicken
Great Napoleon in Russian winter
Distressed chicken cringing, panting:

'Pray, of what use is a man's name
When his head is off his neck?'

Part of a Whole

Help tell blind mortals fighting for God Almighty:
In my neighbour lies something lacking in me
Just as in me lies something lacking in them
In each lies something lacking in others
Everyone being a part of a big orbit.

KHALID IMAM*

I Salute the Bravest of Storms
(For Late Lieutenant Colonel Muhammed Abu Ali)

Brave men are known
Not by the chest they beat
Nor are they crowned by the lies
They told to the hens

True, the earth always tells
With certainty the true sound
Of an elephant's stump

At Baga,
Ask the ants the casualties it suffered
When Abu Ali trampled on its grimy cowardly infidels

No, l shall shed no tears
For a lion that was silenced by traitorous stones

True,
l shall weep not,
For a wind that brought back
Peace to our deserted huts

I shall eternally salute the gallantry
Of lion Abu Ali, the bravest of storms

---

* **Khalid Imam** is a poet and multiple awards–winning bilingual playwright. He is the Vice Chairman of Association of Nigerian Authors Kano state branch and a Board of Trustee Member of Poets In Nigeria.

True,
l shall sing my song only in praise
Of that storm that fed the eyes
Of crushed terrorists with sand of defeat

Yes, tears are rains only for cowards to bath in shame

Oh Ali, l ask: why should l weep for your demise?
Forever, l shall weep not for you
I ask, what do you call the one who mourns a lion, a fool?

Abu Ali, the peace we all enjoy today will be one
Of the juicy fruits you will surely eat in the garden
Only martyrs are welcomed.

Rest in peace, brave soldier!

Maiduguri

Here I am
To pay a homage
To the diligent memories
Of my eloquent ancestors

Here I am
To have a handshake
With the peace permeating all your plains

Now,
A seed of harmony sprouts everywhere,
As if to kiss the sky it soars high like a merry sparrow

Thanks to your gallant resistance
Bravo to your dogged resilience
Kudos to your persistent perseverance

Maiduguri,
Truly peace has a succulent taste of honey.

In the Nest of Tears

We are poor girls
Escaped from the bloody hyenas
Attacking the weak and innocent souls.

Sadly,
We were camped
In the nest of rapists
There, a slice of bread is gold
While hunger is an ocean
And the carefree beasts
Paid to cater for us
Like thievery rodents
In broad daylight
They emptied the granary
To feed their fat siblings
Not belonging to our camps.

What are they if not shameless rapists of teenagers –
Poor girls too infant to mother a child?

What do you call the phony puritan clergymen
In the camps defecating in their places of worship
Or those uncaring hubbies who bribe the guards
To have free sex with their daughters
Or wives in exchange of stolen food?

Where is the safety
We were promised

In this nest of tears
Where beautiful petals are daily torn
By the heartless demons seemingly applauded
By the loud silence of all?

BENJAMIN ARMSTRONG ZUGU*

Maiduguri

Once vibrant with splendour
Eminence crowned your labour
Home of peace to all
The pauper as well as the wealthy
Excelling life's endeavours
Your fame rose high,
And reverberated on the horizon,
Traversing the moon's crescent.

Now faced with chaos and strife,
Your bowels filled to brim,
With the blood of beleaguered souls
Your streets littered with carcasses,
Your inhabitants scattered in quandary
Struggling with hunger, shelterless
The mean harmattan humming
On their naked bodies
!Gbum!! Gbum!!!
Another explosion on their supple bodies.

---

* Benjamin Armstrong Zugu hails from Guma local government in Benue state, and is currently a final year student of English and Literary Studies, University of Maiduguri.

God Deliver Us...

He stared blankly at my conscience
His sunken cheeks and hollow eyes
Gnaw at my heart
His limbs all feeble
His distended stomach
Slouching on its feeble feet.
His mother, a replica
Her ribs stood out like broomsticks
Her spinal cord a sunken ridge
No diagnosis required to bridge
The grieve and the grave.

His siblings, no difference
Their shoulders and elbows
Conspicuous discs and blades
They crouched around him
Sloughed in sorrow.

Wobbly they all trudged on
To escape further attacks
Victims of insurgency and famine.

And I skyward I look
Palms spread and pray
God deliver us from this calamity.

RAZINAT T. MOHAMMED[*]

What will I say?

What will I tell the world happened to me?
What will I tell this child kicking so hard inside of me?
How can my words form on this pallid lips?
How can my eyes show hope for a rising sun?
When my heart carries a burden so heavy it can burst
In my body, flows water and blood, mixed
How can I cry when all I see is my tears?
Are some problems not deserving of bloody tears?
Round the clock, this child kicks and my heart is stilled
Perhaps he is furious that he lies in the wrong bed
What could I do when the times have changed?
And strangeness takes over the land
A son kills his own father and ties the mother to her iron bed
What do you call this phenomenon that has overwhelmed the
    land?
This son who poisoned his brothers because they would not
    tow his line
What can I say about this harvest of woe?

Every home, its own story tell
And so, my house that was home to this monster
Has crumpled to dust, my heath as cold as the dead
I am a woman who gladly suckled her infant in her youth
But must be gagged for a second suckle by an adult?
What is there to tell except of the bleeding of a woman's heart
Hunted by the twist in her fate?

---

[*] **Razinat T. Mohammed** is Associate Professor at the University of Maiduguri. She
is an award- winning creative writer.

If I could speak to this child, I would speak to him about this
world
Perhaps, he too would refuse to see the rising sun that soon
must set
If I could strangle his unformed neck and pull out each
Artery, will my desired solution come?
The ancient upbringing rears its head in a matter of life and
death
'Life is life' its faint whispers sting my subconscious mind
What rights have I to take another's life, yet my humanity has
been taken
Why should I live on, to feel this pangs continue to hit my
fragile ribs?
Yet, my dying is linked to the dying of this child?
That faint whisper rumbles in my head like a bee buzz
'Even of your life, you have no rights what then of your
unformed child?'
What life is this anyway?
When a woman is forced to swallow her own vomits?
When the snake glides out of its skin, does it return to wear it?
Is it expected that a father views the nakedness of his grown
daughter?
Or should a son pleasure himself in the nudity of his mother as
she takes a bath?
These laws are not taught by words of the mouth
Some rights and wrongs of humanity are not uttered yet are
universal
Same in Pakistan, same in China, Czechoslovakia and Yerwa
Tell me then how to pronounce my words to this child when he
comes!

Tell me what I will say to this child who is both a son and a
grandson!!

I Returned

From afar, I saw the land
Lying bare for there was no inhibitions beside the rubbles
Can this be my homeland, my mother's homestead?
Where my cousins and I played hide and seek in youth?
Where is my father's marbled balcony?
The balcony where visitors squatted at his feet to seek counsel
Where is the Cedar table where as a child, I had placed his
    morning tea?
I see a heap of rubble and wonder if that is my uncle's flat.
The beautiful French windows, an idea he brought from his
    travels
Overseas lay scattered in splinters amidst the dusty desert
    sands.
The broken glasses of blue and green reflect the sun's face a
    million times
Can this grey rubble be my father's homestead?
Even the neem tree that stood tall and proud at the entrance
Has a story to tell. Its trunk, deeply serrated and the jagged
    edges
Speak of mutilation done in haste.
The neem tree is Yerwa's identity and could this sacred tree
Not be spared the horror that has befallen its people?
Where do I stand in the mist of all the ruins?
Where do I place my feet to feel the soothing touch of my
    motherland?
What am I to do when the hope of the land lie buried under the
    rubbles.
I have read stories and have watched horrors linked to my
    motherland

The origin of such horrors I cannot fathom
So I returned to demystify this wanton surge of anger
I returned to make meaning of the siege?

My Arrest

What do I know of wars and curfews?
What do I know of the colours of the rainbow?
I am a maid used to washing and cleaning
To help a widow, bring up my siblings.

Can my clothes not be old and torn?
   Could I not walk in rags and have respects?
When the leaders operate an unfair system
Is it my fault that I don't have enough?

Do you beat a child and warn to be still?
Should I not cry when I am robbed and raped of my rights?
What do I know of wars and curfews?
Why do you arrest me for walking on the streets to work and
   earn?
I know not the colours of the rainbow
So why do you talk to me of wars and curfews?

UVIE GIWEWHEGBE*

Haram

Daily they shed
blood without care
the poor and the innocent they flare
Preying on the weak, a coward's tactics, obviously not their
    size

Daily we hear
Seen and confirmed from the news
cuddled in muddled truth
that women and children alike
have no right over life
And Men in camouflage of deceit
Lost in the battle of ignorance and creed

Daily they have it done
carrying out a mission with no vision
like they have sworn to a killing spree
of both the guilty and the free.

Daily,
the act gets fiery
like crazy gods in fury
This ghoulish game
Of politics and God

* Uvie Giwewhegbe has a Master's degree from the Department of English at the University of Lagos. She writes plays and poetry and is the author of *The Man With The White Hat*, a collection of short stories published by Malthouse.

Hardened and swayed
By a Holy Book turned upside down
Daily we crave for a change
To put these weapons at bay
And save the life of bleeding nation
from the daily vices of insecurity and insurgency
distracting all souls from the resources that make us whole

And when we heard Shekau is dead
Killed like he killed
"It will be a relief"
Say those who believe
whose prayers Heaven has blessed
With grace that cannot be seen but with "patience".

Haram! Haram!
The lost voice of Haram!
Time shall come, o yes and soon
that the news will not be you
But a New Nigeria, in greatness and truth.

IDRIS MUSA OKPANACHI*

The Ashes

It began in the river
On the surface of the Sun
Scorching this piece of firing desert below
And the rains fell with AK47
Taller than the people

The innocent colors
Of the rainbow are tainted
With blood in the homestead of Ka'ana
The household once teemed
With bantering teenagers
Whose whereabouts
Are lost in the twilight of the Night

Where would she find their footprints?
On the treacherous silent hot dust?
Where would she see their graves?
Where would she find their bodies?
Even a piece of their clothes
Their nails hair or the snippet
Of anything. Memorabilia. Hurt

---

* **Musa Idris Okpanachi** is an award-winning poet who has published in reputable international journals like *Presence Africaine* (Paris), Kunapipi (Denmark), Pyramids, Iraq Literary Review, and *Ufaham: Journal of African Studies* in the United States. He teaches at Federal University, Dutse.

Why are the rains quiet?
Why is the night not telling the truth?
Why is the day so empty?

Their tales and their shadows
Move quietly around the house
At night knocking on the doors
Ringing the silent bells
Kolo, Mustapha, Babangana and Kyari
Are shuttling playing laughing
In the grave of Ka'ana's memory
Like the dreams in which the earth teems
With lives which empty into the dust
To whom do we bequeath *Liwuram*?

Children of Travellers

Children of travellers lend me
Your tongues without voice
Give me your ears of solitude

You that exist yet not there
I speak through silence to you
I speak through tears and wounds
To you whose being is just a silhouette
I speak through the wind and flutes
I am the piper chronicling the acts
 The undertakers' pickaxes

Wherever you are, come
And be weaved into this poem
At least you could be a stanza
A verse, a word a syllable
Or just a letter that you have become

Those from the hot ashes of war, come
From homes that are pulverized, come
The marabous of the world, come

Oh my orphans your homestead
Has become smoke and mirage
Oh the abandoned ones
Strangers shall inherit you
Come with me, this trip is endless

You do not understand the world
The world is not a place for you
The world has taken away the little it has given you
It has taken everything from you
Even before you are born

It is to you I speak, the ones that squat in the slums
The master of ghetto passing the night
Leaning on the buttresses of trees
The ones that sleep between stones eating droppings

The ones that carry perpetual wounds
And blisters on their hands juggling
With the acts of death in their eyes
The ones ravaged by memories
And are gnawed by hunger

The ones plagued by insomnia
Hunted by the slaughtering
Of their parents before their eyes
And the ones co-opted into war
By the alien guns, it is to you I speak

Children of tattered costumes
My brothers whose mothers
Would never come back
My brother refugees who saw
Whose mothers are raped by the holy rebels
Who saw scars of wars hacking in Sambisa

You are the children of the North East
Where the days and the nights are the same
Where the only companions are vultures
And jackals performing the rites of passage
The Moon and the stars are mere candles and flowers

But our spirit carries the light flying
Above the boundaries of our ancestral homelands
We are ones the same united in our space

We drift in the veldts
We hide and seek with sprites and yetis
We travel with the winds and twilights of blood
We frolic in the Savannah among the graves
Learning the language of jerboas and snakes
We ride roller coasters on the rainbows
Because we are free

Ours is a fate of absolute freedom in constraints
Ours is a world where almost everything is lost
Ours is the purest pleasure of the bliss of mourning
We have short memories we bear no grudges
And because we forget, we are happy

We see no differences between our races
We pass time among sand dunes
Privy to the utmost secrets of the graveless
Sometimes we drink elixir fountains from Alau
Sometimes we rename ourselves
Since our parents have dissolved
Into Blood and the earth

We chum and chant songs
With the eternal mammies of dreams
Eat aquatic delicacy of sweetness
By the edge of the river of blood
That drowned the only people we knew
We drink effervescent love
To gain the energies to dream

We tread the benighted roads
Of sepulchres with no epitaph
Where every grain of sand is a piece of flesh

The merciless Sun scorch our backs
Where the ground is too slippery
The skies have treated us like enemies
It has lead us into the wastelands and fires
Where we break stones with bare hands
Rains have fallen unceasingly with brimstones
Because we are always hungry we eat acids
Drink hemlock and cyanide rehashed from bins

We were never born our parents are
As the jinns and winds gyrating with the sun
We only learn the kindness of a mother from wayfarers
We know charity from strangers and pilgrims
We eat from passersby and lunatics
We learn comradeship and acquaintance
From the corpses lying by the roadside
We learn the protection of a father from butchers
Hangmen, bullies and magicians
We spring from the shins of women
We gestate inside the bark of trees interned in the saps

OLIVE CHINYERE AMAJUOYI*
Cries from the Forest (For Chibok girls)

I can hear the cries of agony
From the dumb tongues in the forest
Held in shattered hopes of freedom
Freedom for the legion of lasses in the forest

I can feel their urge to clean up
For the stink of their period makes them vomit
But buckets are far from pool and well
And the beasts of the forest know no shower

I can see their darting eyes
Through thick cobwebs in the forest
They seek and search for escape routes
Perhaps opportunity might come calling

I can hear them groan in pain
As their mother's cry echo in the forest
They crave and long for freedom
But alas, uncertainty beclouds the face of the sun

---

* **Olive Chinyere Amajuoyi** is a writer whose major focus is Poetry and fiction. She has written over 100 articles and essays either published on her website: idealolive.blogspot.com or presented as a speech. She lives and works in Enugu, Nigeria.

We are not safe

Even in broad day light
Our own sun seems to be covered
Freaked out and plundered,
We were laid to be slaughtered
For Sambisa beasts to toast and feast
What greater plague can befall
The heroines of mother earth?
And what manner of crime is it to be a woman?

We are not safe in the day
Neither are we safe in the night
We are not safe in the schools
Neither are we safe in worship places
The perfume of despair and death has filled our air
At the peak of their womanhood
Our girls were marooned as sex slaves
What manner of crime is it, to be a woman?

Ode to Leah Sharibu

Like a rattling rumour it became true
Heralded by the wind and made our ears jingle
That Leah shook hands with Martyrs of old
Hence died a thousand times to rise up stronger
Not minding, not thinking, the crown of thorns ahead
Should we tell her tale like a fairy tale?
Her name is Leah, the teenage Amazon

Like the biblical Israelis of faith
She was defiant amid the raging beasts
That roared to make her bow
To the god of spears and arrows
Like others, she desired freedom but gave it up
To secure a treasure wrapped up in rags
Her name is Leah, the teenage Amazon

ADAMA Y. BALLA YERIMA[*]

Standstill. . .

Ya Allah my hands are up high
My eyes rolled up high
Looking at the crescent of Rajab
My tongues silently reciting the *Iqlas*

I woke from my slumber
Picked my Nokia 110
Dialled my Al-Rayyan's number
Call not allowed

Ya Allah! See us through this standstill
Maiduguri is at a stand still WhatsAPP, no Facebook
No forward, no backward,
Only Allah knows for how long

Oh how long will I wait to talk to my Al-Rayyan?
Oh how long will I wait to do my forex trading?
Oh how long will I wait to surf the net?
Oh how long will I wait to BBM, WatsApp, Facebook, and
    Twitter?

Ya Allah let our standstill situation be our last sacrifice
Towards the restoration of peace in our violated Borno
Ya Allah look into our hearts, see our tears eyes
Ya Allah only you can do it

---

[*] **Adama Balla Yerima** was born on December 19, 1974 in Maiduguri, Borno State. She was afflicted by polio as an infant and suffers severe disabilities. Despite her physical challenges, she has authored two books, a collection of poetry and a play. She is the founder of Zadaya-Kanen Polio Disabilities Initiative and now works as social mobilization officer of the National Primary Health Care Development Agency (NPHCDA). She is married and lives in Maiduguri

No JTF
No dialogue
No amnesty
No retreat
No surrender
But only *Allah, ya Allah* can do it, *ya Allah* has done it.
Ya Allah will do it again, am sure of that
Allah will soon decree Borno to be the home of peace
And peaceful it shall be.

Amen

Terrorist

Your awkward face lurking in
    The quagmire of nightmare
Of blindfolded wrapped in ignorance

    You are still around
    And so you wish to be
I do not know for how long

    You have no religion, no faith

    You are neither human, nor beast
    your are just a quagmire.

.

ABUBAKAR A. OTHMAN

The Legacy Gardens of Borno

Its now a legacy in Borno
That politicians build public homes with public funds
And keep them away from public while in office
For the nocturnal luxury of their sorcerers
The invisible occupants of the legacy gardens of Borno.

In Maiduguri ghosts are more important than teachers
The IDPs would inhabit Teachers estates
While the legacy gardens of the politicians
Yawn with emptiness
Reserved for use by ghosts
The nocturnal guests
Of the politician

For the love of history, note:

The legacy began with the Architect-politician
Builder of 202 units unallocated in office
Reserved for nocturnal habitation
By the fetish totems of the politician.
He left behind 303 more units for his sorcerers
The sinister source of his office,
Only his exit restored occupancy
To the homeless citizens of the state
Left unsheltered by the politician.

His successor the business vampire
Owner of the golden gate empire,
Whose tenure had 707 units untenanted
And a thousand more unallocated
Reserved for the ghosts and goblins
Nocturnal providers of treasures
And blood nourishment for the politician.

His protégé the landlord-politician
Owner of every nook and cranny in the state
Though more inclined to luxury than sorcery
Kept the legacy of invisible tenancy
For the luxury of his totems
And privacy with his *tchotchkes*
The invisible occupants of
The legacy Gardens of Maiduguri.

Trembling Night

The bombs blast
The dogs bark
The night rumbles like thunder
Trembling up children in deep sleep

I perch on the edge of the bed
Wakeful to another long night
Of tremors and terrorists

A restless city of fleeing residents
A sleepless night of fleeting images
Of corpses floating like floes
In the blood streams of the streets.

Corpses whose eyes have refused to close
Whose mouths have remained agape;
They are also sleepless like me.

We keep vigil over the city
For the rendering of these conspiracies
Of murdering by the state and the terrorists
In the name of God and country.

The Date Fruits of MARKAS

In the madras of Markas
We learn the metaphor of life
Through the images of dates
The death resistant fruit of the desert,
Dry dates for the jihadists
Fresh dates for the infidels,
The incomprehensible logic
Of the nihilists' ideology.

Like their fellow murderers in power
Feeders of the poor with flesh food and blood
The nihilists of Markas feed their followers
With dry dates of falsehood
About a God that relishes flesh and blood
Promising paradise for murderers.

At the gate of Markas
We came across a hawker
With a sackload of fresh dates
The yellowish-brown flesh of the fruits
Gave us appetite for fresh life,

The bystanders understand us
Urging us for the taste of the fresh dates
Shielding us from the dry date of death
The charmed food of the murders.

ABDULSALAM El-MUBASHIR*

Girl Bomber

She was too young to understand
The task she was asked to undertake
The innocence of age 12
Maybe 13 or 14

She was unspoilt and uneducated
The one government and society neglected
Left vulnerable to evil
An easy prey for the devil
That lurks in street corners.
A promising teenage girl
Denied the nutritious food of books
 Made a ready crude for crooks.

And when the promises of good life
She was betrayed,
 The promises of good life in heaven
She became attracted to

Dressed up in explosives
Set off on a mission destructive
Her own life inclusive
She became a victim of her innocence
From the deceit of the two ends.

---

* **Abdulsalam El Mubashir** is a Nigerian creative writer.

For the Kidnapped Chibok Girls

In a state under the rule of emergency
Replete with checkpoints by the military
Over 270 innocent girls
Were carted away by diabolized puritans
Acting on the orders of Satan

Their leader dressed in a dreadful turban
And calls himself Shekau
Who says western education is abhorrent, 'haram'
But on him are gadgets and ammunition

Perhaps worse is the ignominious inaction
Of the leaders of a nation
That left her daughters unprotected
In a state so violently infested

The post-abduction actions
Are nothing but ruse regrets
A spurious assurance of protection
To the entire population
A theatrical cry on television

Kerchief in trembling hands
Clearly an act for all
Dabbing the tearless eyes
Both shameful acts of lies
To mop the true cry;
#Bring back our girls now and alive

ABUBAKAR M. JODA[1]

Explosion in Arewa

When the serene earth gets broken
The azure sky fractures
And heavens fall down
In a boom like thunder
Humans fly in flakes
 pieces of flesh scattered,
Arewa fluxes like an abattoir
Flooded with foul secretions,
Our huts collapse apart
In the mosques, the flames
Whirling against the azure skies
Human flesh dangling
 Reeking odour
What have we done to deserve this?
This North of ours decays to a morgue
We see this calamity on TV
Now on our threshold it happens.

---

[1] **Abubakar Muhammad Joda** is a student of pharmacy at Gombe State University, Gombe State. He has a passion for short fiction and poetry.

ANITA JACOB*

In Sambisa

A light flickers from a long concealed match
Footsteps are heard
The flicker is doused
The match quickly concealed

The little one is groaning again
Her first mark of womanhood has come
In this madhouse
But this place is not a house
This mad forest

This must be the evil forest
The one of which *Uwar* told
In her lilting voice, in the ancient story
Of seven heads on one shoulder
Dancing trees and chuckling tortoise
Of a beautiful girl.
That unheeded all advice
And falls victim
Of a ghost with borrowed limbs.

This evil forest
This persistently dark place
Has not the evil spirits

---

* **Anita Jacob** is from Abia State, Nigeria. She is a final year student at the Department of English and Literary Studies, Niger Delta University, Amassoma, Bayelsa State. She is a blogger.

The kind of which *Uwar* told
The spirits of Sambisa forest
Look like human
One head, two malevolent eyes
Two legs that aim for the ribs
Two hands that grope for grub
And a body bound in throes
Throating *Insha Allah.*

MUJTABA S. ABUBAKAR*

Don't Worry

Don't worry
I get that all the time
I even pushed my motorcycle
Miles apart from my meal
It was 9:00 pm
And all the roadblocks were blocked

By another month,
We wouldn't have to be paid
Our salaries would be invested.
Never mind

I bombed INEC offices,
Newspaper houses, and
A couple of churches
And luckily, all the forces
Were busy taxing drivers.
Just kidding

---

* **Mujtaba S. Abubakar** is a Nigerian creative writer

OFOKO OGECHI*

Can't You for a Moment Rest, Mosquito Boys?

Buzzing mosquitoes
That trouble all night long
When peace and rest are needed
Sucking the blood of the innocents
And never desire to stay at peace

Unwelcomed visitor
You always visit at night
When you are not needed
Coming and going as if you own the house
You come through the door
Through the window
Through every slits and crevices of our house

Unto us you were born
Unto us you survive
You are mosquito
You are the king of terror

From the East we saw you
From the West we heard you coming
From the South you made your way
From the North your steps tremble
As we remember the voice that says
Birth in hell in the land of Judas
You are by no means the least of the leading city of the Giant

---

* **Ofoko Oghechi** is a Nigerian creative writer

From you will come a terrorist
Who will terrify my people

In the beginning was the sword
And the sword was with you
All terror was made through it
And you took flesh of horror and dwelt among us
By the desert side like baby lion
You stay while we wept
On your neck you hang your irons
And requires song form us
Song of tears
The sound of bitter weeping
Mother is crying for her children
She refuses to be comforted for they are dead

Like the Egyptians you torment us
Like Babylonians you suppress us
You stand on our way like the Goliath
Seeking for our lives like Herod
As you demanded our head like the Herodias

Even though you walk through the valley
You fear no evil
For the Babas are with you
On their hands they breed you up

I will rise and have no pity on flesh
Oh! Our flesh has suffered violence
And through violence you have sucked our blood
In our distress we cry to you

As we lift up our eyes to the hills
When our nets could not save us
Behold, as the eyes of the servant
Look to the hand of their master
We tearfully asked; cant you for a moment rest,
Mosquito boys!

IQUO DIANAABASI EKE*

To Survive the War

Order a beer and spiced meat,
watch the razing of whole villages,
shake your weary head,
shrug your secure shoulders,
wish the northerners well.

Four years post Chibok
argue that it is a farce still,
propaganda from the opposition, to
undermine the government of your brother
from another tribe in the south.

Hear of flags hoisted in the North East,
claim this is karma, served hot,
for the death of your brothers and
sisters decades away.

Laugh off Mubi, Baga, Bama, Gwoza,
say '*Na dem-dem, e no konsain us!*'
flip the channel, seek Serie A, La Liga,
EPL & Champions league on Supersport,
order some peppersoup,

---

* **Iquo Diana Abasi Eke** writes prose, poetry and scripts for radio and screen. Her first collection of poems was shortlisted for the NLNG Nigeria prize for literature, and the ANA poetry prize; both in 2013.It was also shortlisted for the Wole Soyinka Literature Prize, 2018. She lives in Lagos.

Write off Dapchi,
Argue about Leah,
'How are we sure the abductions happened'?
Claim it was all staged to make the
government appear to be working.
Shout yourself hoarse at the killing
of a Christian evangelist.
Raise hell only when churches
are bombed in the north, look away
when the victim is a non-Southerner.

Grimace at the execution of Leman,
Ask no one in particular
'These people are still at it?'
learn some *shaku-shaku*,
keep the hustle on full throttle.

One half of Nigeria may be in a chokehold,
but you club hard and stay 'woke'.
people may fear to travel or farm
from village to village, but for you,
life on cruise control is no adage

The Staccato Was No Firework

The staccato from afar was too
violent to be New Year day fireworks,
drawing out fear so palpable it
left her impaled for the longest seconds.

Then, the baby was strapped to her back,
Then, a snack and water were tied in a cloth
and tossed over her shoulder,
then, the race began,
then her feet took off,
unaware they wore no shoes.
Then the fires wheezed past her,
and the screams propelled her faster,

Then, an unearthly smell hit her;
charring skin mingled
with burning grains,
then, the noise stopped, time
suspended, and Dooshima discovered ...
This staccato in Guma was no firework,
but a bullet to her eye.

The guard gave his word,
not to fight for or against livestock,
but to defend the integrity of his people,
for if visitors respected grazing laws of the land,
there would be peace,
then indigenes, cattle, herdsmen and
even land would not suffer;
equity would exist in all dealings.

Taking to duty post that night,
he worried neither about wife,
nor about son's impressive drawings,
nor about secondary school-bound daughter.
Dawn would soon come
then he would travel home for late celebrations.

The guard's vow was sealed with
uniform and cutlasses;
but his blades, though sharp, were
no match for the marauders' guns.
Then with a bullet to the back
the guard learnt too late,
the staccato in Logo was no fiesta.
The staccato was the deafening soundtrack
to the New Year day massacre.

Centenary Condolences

Condolences my country, Condolences.

A hundred tears for your hacked men and women,
another hundred for your youths
whose blood colour your streets
crimson at your centenary anniversary,

A hundred more tears for your leader
who goofs an ill-planned strumming,
while your underbelly burns.
Condolences, Nigeria.

A thousand tears for your daughters,
never to return whole;
     or sane

A hundred tears for dusk time games
never again to be enjoyed
after the dance into captivity

Two-Three-Four nameless
  The value, not the sequence,
      Two-Three-Four, faceless
        girls, not the country code
Condolences,
A hundred salutes for the country
that once was...
a dream merger of unfamiliar neighbours
whose values straddle this funeral pyre,

Ahmed. Katung. Dooshima
   ... Condolences
For the hand which stretched too eager for blood
but never to mend this broken fence

Segun.Dike. Osahon.
   ... Condolences
For tears, dried too soon on sore cheeks
and a heart, scabbed raw
while revenge festers in the
implacable half of a yellow sun

Effiom. Wanemi. Itohan.
   ... Condolences
for the black pearls they ripped from your belly
and left you hungry in the midst of plenty
....Condolences

The funeral procession is ablaze
with flares of despair
To where will you run?
How long can you hide?

Can you douse these flames of hate
with waters of ethnic diversity?
Will this fallow land ever
recover from these ashes?

Home remains a distant
yearning for the exile,
yet this bird too must
perch after flight,

Condolences Nigeria,
Condolences!

Love wears many faces

Love wears many faces,
speaks myriad tongues,
walks crooked paths in different guises.
Espy her beneath the many garbs;
Wrapped in a shield of *hijabs*,
hushed voices and bubbly laughter,
Amina shares her lunch with Mary,
because innocence knows not friend or infidel,

The farmer knows not the specifics of recession,
but she minds not her deepening wrinkles
nor her griping stomach, with each missed meal,
long as the steadily shrinking
garri can go round her children.
She sucks in the pain and lack,
and reproduces it as an untiring smile,
love thinks not of self, but of the loved.

At the cry of a new born,
friends and foe break into ululation,
prayers for abundance and good health,
hatchets buried under heaps of baby powder.
This untainted expression of love
Is primeval, quintessential,
This love is the patent marker of our primordial beginnings.

To patiently guide that child
or subordinate though others have
moved to the next lesson,
to deny that child a favour, so they

learn a lesson in self-reliance,
this too is love speaking,
though her voice may be harsh.

I was raised by a village
when a child belonged to everyone,
if you harmed one, you harmed us all...
that was love, before we learnt to dissect
ourselves as religious fractions
and tribal inequalities.

Before our sisters and neighbours
became 'those people,'
before Yoruba degenerated to *Atorouduangufok*
before all northerners turned *EwuHawusa*,
and Igbos became *Nyammiri,*
before *aboki* went from friend to fool,
and we could no longer tell the difference.

At birth we learn not tears or laughter,
but respond to hunger and joy by default,
for we all belong to one tribe: Human.
Despite skin colour, tribe, class,
religion or even sect,
original, devoid of external coatings,
we all understand one language: LOVE
her essence pure, her tone unchanged.

SU'UR SU'EDDIE VERSHIMA AGEMA*

The Waiter of the Skull

Vultures in circle smiling
Hyenas all around cackle
Prowling where men once stood

Silence is a companion that holds everyone close
Peace for the muted and fallen
Silence for the souls of those dying alive
Amidst the noise that becomes the waiter's song

Bombs are the firecrackers
Celebrating feast of human flesh
Blown for breakfast
Bullet-riddled bodies for lunch
Dinner is a potpourri of blood, flesh and bones
Tears is served as the meal in-between
Grief the plate on which these are served

Death is the waiter
Serving drinks drawn from veins
Vinegar on hyssops
For the saved and despised
Everyone sips, slowly
Fear the stick taking it to the lips

Will they be remembered in paradise tonight?

* **Su'ur Su'eddie Vershima Agema** is an editor, an award-winning author and development worker. He has four poetry collections, a children's book and a short story collection. He blogs at http://sueddie.wordpress.com.

Nightmares Raised on the Fringes

In our nightmares, lived through dawning dusks
existence is governed by devils that tune evil
owls hoot trumpets of doom
bullets refine the state of the nation
bunkers are permanent holdings
grenades the *shot put* used to pursue glory

Leagues of fallen angels assemble at plants
to surprise suited apes dressed in colonial robes
as rigs fall, crashing on the back of the giant eagle
its wings plucked by depleting barrels whose weights lose
    value with a dropping dollar

Marshlands send signals to Northern cabals
fights for cultural heirlooms are restarted on sensible and
    senseless plains
in the name of brazen gods and dying men
hunger become an arsenal that fuel freedom fighters, crusaders
    and jihadists
daughters and mothers *back* bombs strapped in place of kids
ladles are replaced with Uzis, AK47s, Danes and SMGs

In the ashes of fallen fathers, twenty children rise
waiting to be dropped by shots that should have saved them
martyrs robed as rebels by powers that be in the *Arsehole* Rock

TOLANI SALAWU*

When Is The End?

Religious persecution, Attitude of hate
   Tortured souls, Insanity normalized
   Oppressed society the order of the day
   When is the end?

Our homes are drowned in flood of blood and tears
   Our children are faced with uncertain future
   When is the end?

They come from jungles
   They shout, shoot and loot
   Then come bigger forces from cities
 More cries, more groans and carnage
When is the end?

Those on higher grounds watch it all with relish
   They cluck and cackle while our homes
Drown in flood of blood and tears
   When is the end?

---

* **Tolani Salawu** is a Marriage Counsellor, an inspirational writer, a philanthropist and advocate of Good Life for the Girl Child and a member of Association of Nigerian Authors. Tolani has written over one hundred articles on attitudes and lifestyles.

ADAMA H. IDRISU*

A Day of Tears

The operation news summoned tears
anxious to stream down, unrestrained.
I stood, yet fell back,
I wish pain can be shared
to weaken the unwanted guest.
I stood, yet crashed back,
the bullet extraction takes eternity.
While supplicating the invisible hand
tapped Nasseh out of anaesthetic sleep,
while praying that Gilead's balm
jostle him back to the race of life.
I received a call,
another heart-rending call
from an artless tongue;
stranger to the art of breaking news.
I stood but slumped back,
when I heard mum and granny
sought refuge in the lion's den.
I stood but crashed back,
when I learnt the strong youths
that escaped terrorists' bullets
have fallen, crippled by hunger
I stood, yet fell flat,
since the day has declared itself

---

* **Adama H. Idrisu** is a Chief Lecturer at Mohammed Goni College of Legal and Islamic Studies Maiduguri. She has published poems in International Poets and World Poetry.

a day of tears,
a day that opened the eyes
as lids to springs of tears.

SAFIYA ISMAILA YERO*

My Northeast Dream

Farmer:
My Northeast dream is to
Till the soil not souls
Bury seeds not corpses,
I dream of a heart that hails
The sight of a sprouting crop
Not fall at the sight of a corpse,
I want to see a boom in farm produce
Not the booming of the bomb
Pupil:
My Northeast dream
Is to hurry to school
In the early morning
After a cup of hot pap
My North East Dream
Is for a land of scholars
To go to school in peace
And walk back home with friends
 amidst merry chatter
and sniff the air spiced
with the aroma of mother's cooking
my Northeast dream
Full of food and people
Mother, father, siblings and family.
My Northeast dream is to sleep in peace

---

* **Safiya Ismaila Yero** is a poet and author of When There is Life. She currently works at the University of Abuja.

And not be haunted by maimed bodies
Floating in streams of blood.
Or deafening grenades
Housewife:
My Northeast dream
Is to bathe my kids at the first cock crow
And dress them for school
Bid their father farewell as he leaves for work
I want to clean and cook and wash and dress and wait
To welcome them with open arms
And watch them devour the afternoon food amidst mild chatter
I want to see my husband home again
I want to hold my two little boys close again
I hear they now know how to shoot with guns
My boys who found a hoe too heavy to lift
Now assemble magazines with glee
I want to hold my little girl again
I should have hidden her in the ceiling
Instead of beneath the bed from whence taken
I wailed she wailed as they dragged her away
And made her wife
My little girl with buds on her chest
My little girl who couldn't tie her wrapper well....
I wish life was a VCR
With a functional rewind button
Rewind...edit...delete...some parts of us

RACHEL MSENDOO KAASE*

Beasts were Babies

Amidst the lightning he strikes
That sparks and lights
A house on fire with four:
Father, mother, daughter; son,
I recall it all.

Amidst the thunder he blows
That leaves debris of corpses
With no one to count the losses
But my tear which flows,
I recall it all.

Amidst the flood he releases
Drowning some, leaving some
With incurable heart diseases
I saw this, disbelieving,
And recalling it all.

Recalling the sun in May
To rise and shine again
Easing me of this dark pain.
Remembering he was clay
    In my hand to hold and mould
    To keep warm in days cold,
    Yaro na,* my gold.

---

* **Rachel Msendoo Kaase** is a Nigerian creative writer.

* *my boy/son*

Recalling the merry moon
Which left us so soon.
Remembering nights
When he was truly mine
And together we did dine
On his laughter and my smile.
Later on to lie on a bed not big
Yet worthy of a king.
Then midnights
When his cry did ring
　　I let him nestle in milky nest
　　Providing him bosomic rest
Just hoping and praying
　　He would turn out best.

Recalling it all
Changes nothing at all
He now stands famously tall
　　While I stoop low in shame
　　For although I can call his name
"Abu"
　　I can never ask "How are you?"
　　Nothing can be the same.
So I continuously recall
My baby being small
The memories are remedies
That bring no cure
But I know for sure
That amidst everything he has done wrong
Once upon a time,
He was my sweet baby boy.

GEORGE CHUKWU*

Dear Falmata

War has broken out on our soil
The people are dressed in red
The north holds their head
Their feet in the south
And both arms of my people
Lay in the east and west

Though life itself is scared to death
I still remember your oval face
Your voice people heard pleading
When men took you fleeing
Your parents eat tears, Falmata
They sigh and sob, "Oh Falmata!"

Who would have thought that
A day like this would come?
When our day turns to night
And weeping becomes music
When blood is the only colour
And death our true comforter

---

* **George Chukwu** is a freelance writer. He has written articles for blogs and websites in different niches but mainly on personal development. He has written over 200 articles for his clients and fellow writers. He is working on his novel and lives at Ojota, Lagos State.

With grief, I write to heads of men
Who hold the yam and knife
Young flesh are missing
In all of our houses
Our minds will have no rest
Until we bring back Falmata

Inertia

While we played with words in cities
Our children were taken away
While we mentioned names of gods
Our girls were eaten without sauce
And Chibike blamed Ajibike
Till the black sheep melted into the night

We held our roots so close
And shone the teeth on the screen
While our houses went up in flames
And western life public defamed
And Chibike blamed Ajibike
Till the black sheep melted into the night

Saidu boasted he came for slaughter
Threatened our fathers, mocked our mothers
And like a king, took our virgins
While we played with words in cities
And Chibike fought Ajibike
Till the black sheep melted into the night

We got a promise from our fathers
And thought they understood our woes
Our fighters cannot push the enemy
For we have Judases among us
Because Chibike blamed Ajibike
Till the black sheep melted into the night

LINDA JUMMAI MUSTAFA*

The Last Meal

Clinking my spoon in my bowl,
I wait earnestly for a meal;
with a heart pounding loudly in my ears,
The night before; I had run twenty-one miles on my own
 not minding the several thorns on my path.
A mother so afraid of death, I left my children to die
at the hands of heartless men of war.
Now as I stare at my unwashed bowl
 with no rice, no maize grits and nor millet gruel
My babies' bodies all blown apart
I wonder how a wicked heart like mine stays alive
 to eat a bitter meal of a lizard's bile.
Clinking greedily my spoon in my bowl, half full, half empty
 without a conscience at all of my lonely escape.
I cry every night like a wounded leopard, loudly and terribly
all too broken to face another day
 my tears run down my face to make a puddle
of regret, of shame, of dejectedness and of gratitude.
when I remember Fatu, Iliya, Gumsu, Hauwa and Zayad
all nourishing the soil or a scavenger's belle I cry

My last meal can't be eaten
the clinking sound of my spoon scraping the bowl tells me that
    my last meal is all in vain
when I have no children, no husband, no family.

---

* **Linda Jummai Mustafa** currently teaches at Ibrahim Badamasi Babangida University, Lapai, Niger State.

II

As I wonder how unfair the world has been to me,
I see others in tattered clothes; men unshaven and raggedy
women smelling from long absence of warm baths.
I wait for a while to see how they eat
their last meal like mine that is cold, dry and tasteless.
They wait in line to be served by strangers a meal all soiled
    with many tears.
They walk silently like ghosts
 remembering their friends, foes and fiery gunmen
 tataaring their guns with no care as many fall to their deaths.
On the queue to a stranger who does not know how hurt we all
    are
a woman runs from nowhere to the table.
Half naked, half alive, half greedy
My child, my mother, my father, my husband
She waves her hands to the sky and back again at us
shooting an imaginary gun at us, *Tararararararararararara!*
She says as we all fall down to avoid her bullets.
I am finished! I am finished!! I am Finished!!! All my people are
    dead!
The crazy woman from nowhere is not crazy at all
her sadness keeps her spellbound at how we walk leisurely to
    take our last meal.
She crawls on all four as we watch studiously how she paddles
over imaginary lengths of grounds: avoiding landmines and
    holes.
Then she latches at a bewildered broken man claiming he had
    raped her to hell and back
but the man cried in horror; shouting earnestly

"I am not the one, I can never be the one we are this way
    because of them."
She abandons him for another as she crawls up to a stranger
    who looked on at this drama
never saying a word or intervening but her urge
to have a revenge so fades away as she lurches to the table
to get her meal of chaos to settle her grumbling stomach and
    shaking hands.
As we all look forward to a last meal of broken pride
 I am happy that I am not like that crazy woman
 at least I still have clothes on and take a bath while we all look
    out for them.
Yet my last meal must not be eaten in a hurry
for I have made up my mind to battle every violent man and
    every violent concept.
For my children, for my husband, for my family
and for my new friends met in camp far away from my home.
I will fight to the last to get me a meal that is fit for the king
even though it shall be my last meal.

DANIEL YOHANNA*

I Want to Learn

Laziz
I want to learn the Arabic language
So that I can listen to the voices
Lamenting in Arabic the domesticated war
That crept into their sieged homestead.
Laziz
I want to learn the Arabic language
So that I can sing dirge-of-love
To the heart broken captives of *yerwa*
Whose spouses are slain by the infidels
Professing faith.
Laziz
I want to learn the Arabic language
So that I may seek the faces of those gods-of-war
That lured our innocent youth
They initiated into Boko-Boys of terror.
Laziz
I want to learn Arabic language
So that I can tour the Middle East,
I want to live there with the voices in *khandaq*
And hear of their horrible tales of domestic-war
That spread into the Boko Haram woes
Here in our land of peace.
Laziz
`I want to learn the Arabic language

---

* **Daniel Yohanna** hails from Cham district, Balanga L.G.A of Gombe State Nigeria. He has a flair for poetry and novels. His stage name is Nature.

So that *Chalifah*, John and *Mustapha*
Will hear the dirge in my voice wafting
The enigmas of dwellers and soldiers slaughtered here in
    kanem empire.

I Wish to See You Again

I hid in a *khandaq* with my gun beside me
Waiting for my fate as a soldier.
I hid in that *khandaq* among corpses
With my gun beside me like my wife.
I hid from the infidels
Who made our wives widows
And made our children orphans
Who stole from our virgins their dignity
And profaned the words "God is great".

I hid there in that *khandaq*
My heart weeping for you
Searching for you among the corpses
Slaughtered for their faith

I brought out your picture from my chest pocket
I being a poet facing my fate,
I held it before my eyes
And said a prayer the poet-teacher taught me.
I kissed your picture with hope
To see you once again my love in *aljen*
For you have always been my *aljenna.*

Where is Our Patriot?

If you see the patriot
Tell him *indawatu* but we are not *klewasile,*
His house is on fire
Burning like the forest in harmattan

If you see the patriot
Tell him the aged couldn't run
To the mountain for refuge,
And the lucky ones at the mountain
Died from the stampede.

If you see the patriot
Tell him *Baga* is silted in blood
No more *Banda* for protein

If you see the patriot
Tell him the man who seats
At his royal fortress is a gobbling
Mumbling in wilted wit

If you see the patriot
Tell him to send us the rain
For the moon, stars and sun to reign
And for his seeds
To germinate and perforate.
If you see the patriot
Tell him to send a dove to *Yerwa*
Let the city look like the giraffe
With the nature of a gazelle.

Notes: *khandaq* is an Arabic word for Trench, *Indawatu* is a Kanuri word meaning good morning while *klewasile* means fine. *Yerwa* is the Kanuri name for Borno State.

JACK VINCENT*

Yerwa

Sun-baked Savannah, where the Sahel
Let out burning flames from the heat of hell.
In Maiduguri, the sun
And the gun
Duelled to death in a desire
To spit out fire;
The harbinger of rage
In a misguided age.

---

* **Jack Vincent** was born and raised in Maiduguri, northeast of Nigeria. He is a trained journalist with specialty in humanitarian access and negotiations. He is the current Secretary of the Association of Nigerian Authors (ANA), Borno State Chapter.

Darkness

Darkness has fallen upon us
And our light is dimmed
By emissaries of the unknown
Prowling the night
Unseen; devouring our barn
Of innocence.

Oh Divine Providence,
Behold our arid faces
Divorced from grace unstudied;
And cupped in the dancing hands
Of a contrite heart.

May the day break;
May our day break.

TANURE OJAIDE*

Fortunately
(from "The Maiduguri Suite")

It rains torrents here too as it does elsewhere.
Defiant winds buffet and drench all in the open.
No echoes of big guns that used to shake from far;
fear and booms have faded away for real thunder.
Fortunately, it rains as it should this time of the year
from deep in the night to dawn and cooling tempers,
swathing partners in the warmth of huddled bodies.
So fortunately, they have encores, covers, and kisses.
Everywhere succumbs to what is due in time and place;
everybody falls for the charm of one thing or person.
Deprivations ravish homes; a filled market of denials.
Unpaid salaries run across multiple states; not just here.
Pickpockets, muggers, and prostitutes pursue their living.
Fortunately, the University Garden thrives with activities—
condoms litter everywhere and you mind your business;
folks seek to fill themselves first before anything else.
There's hide-and-seek of young and old; love-hunting—
public prohibition is no deterrence to overheated desires.
Fortunately, there are tears as well as laughter; many gone
as so many left now to harvest crops of the exhausted soil.
Passersby press streets despite army trucks and convoys.
Squabbles of lenders and debtors drag many to court.
Uproar in open rivalries in the harem; cries for sharing
more intense than ever. Calls for prayers deafen ears.

---

* **Tanure Ojaide** is a writer of poetry, fiction, and non-fiction. He is also a professor of Africana Studies at the University of North Carolina at Charlotte

And generous gestures surprise one after the degeneration.
They live their part here, leave others to their worldliness.
I had heard of carnage but the rains wash away the crimson.
I see perforated buildings; plasterers restoring Ground Zero.
Fortunately, I experience cuddling rain from night to dawn.

He Was One of Us, Shekau

And he had played football with age-mates
now testifying to his transformation into a grisly rodent,
had savoured *banga* soup like a native connoisseur,
and so had keen appetite for the delicacies life provides.
At some time he had taken the same path as others;
their company a boisterous conversation of young men.
Then his Almighty was everybody's non-discriminating
patriarch you prayed to for forgiveness over missteps;
the One who dispensed grace with both hands to penitents.
He had dodged house chores to play football and with
transparent lies covered for fellow youths out in the field.
He would not smash a roach, mosquito, or fly, many testify.
"He was one of us, playing and looking for a stable bearing."
Now the gory stream he exacts on the land frightens;
his bombs and guns shatter peace into fragmented bodies
and only he and his cabal of believers have a right to live.
At what time in his dream life did he shed normalcy
for the savagery of barbarians offering human sacrifice?
When in the day did he throw out his embroidered kaftan
for a black gown and hood over his face turned stolid?
And yet he had played football with age-mates
he abandoned for the disquieting call from darkness;
had devoured *banga* soup as if that was what he would
desire in heaven as reward for his prudence and faith,
and taken the same safe path as others in his company.
"He was one of us, playing and looking for a stable bearing."
Now confined to the bush, the black rodent, mortal terror
of the Sahel, ambushes humans to soak the soil with blood
to make a pointless point of irrational judgement on faith.

Now who had been a fisherman floods everywhere red
and scares the world with his bloodletting animal capers;
once so human he had played and scored goals to applause,
voraciously consumed *banga* dish he knew through friends,
and followed the same safe paths beyond the pale of police
as those he now sees as outcast ones he wants to wipe out
of the very earth that had made him happy and now waits
for however long to catch him for the ultimate judgment.
He was well with others on the same side of life before
crossing; possessed by nebulous Sambisa Forest djinns.
"He was one of us, playing and looking for a stable bearing."

Tashan Bama

All vibrant, it defies logic of a troubled scene—
a quilt of colours and a collision of aromas
that would diminish Samarkind's market pride.
Pagnes, boubous, kaftans, and all that make Borno
a crossroads of the Sahel; mass movement all over.
In place of an evacuated market straddling Bama Road,
a throng that defies the logic of a vast battleground.
A press of humans, djinns in human figures, bombers,
militia men, women, and youths clothed in festive
fabrics in a rolling stream that bears all in one wave.
Keke-ful, the town moves on however irregularly;
no *okadas* and that ban relief and threat to the column
but foists on the public a population of brainless drivers.
Here the disabled breaks through despite the challenges;
an explosion of mansions cancels out perforated homes.
Tashan Bama*—filling aroma of fruits, oil, and spices;
assembly of Sahel's wealth; beauty of regional tribes,
you have sucked in from everywhere who seek refuge;
a beehive as no other I have seen of a battleground.
This defies logic: the beauty remains despite pockmarks;
the beauty still there in peace despite gunshots and bombs
of those flying a black flag over the fortune of a nation.
Tashan Bama, you defy the logic of war and peace,
disability and growth cohabiting in a restive market.
Despite publicized suicide bombers, virgins in *hijab*,
and boys too timid to know why they carry bombs,
the city lives on, bigger, hardly quiet, and thriving.

RUTH BARIKI*

Boko Haram

Let education stop, they say.
Let science go into extinction,
    Let the west go to hell,
        Boko Haram.

        Let our towns not develop,
        Let the buildings come down
        For they are a symbol of western education.
    Boko Haram.

    We must play the jihadists.
    Boko must stop
        So they say
        Boko is haram.
        So they say.

But why do they use
The scientist's bomb.
Why do they visit the cities?

Tell me
Is Boko
Really Haram?

---

* **Ruth Bariki** has just completed her Master's program in the Department of English at the University of Lagos.

PART II

THE DIALOGUE POEMS

HYELADZIRA BALAMI[*]

The Markas, Site Not Seen in Maiduguri, June 2018
(for A.O. and T.O.)

You fell short -- with your halt -- of making the Markas
Our next World Heritage Site
Because you chose flight over fight!

You who have been to the Tower Eiffel and the KLCC Towers
You who have been to the height of the Statue of Liberty
Weren't so liberated from fear after all!
Nor was your trip to Madagali's Sukur ever so sullied with fear,
Righteous or sacrilegious

When I decided because I could to take you to the Markas
For an inaugural visit
I had to make a swift U-turn with the Sienna
Because you shrieked for a detour
As you both sweated in the mortuary-cold SUV, demurring and
    kicking...

And Abubakar Othman made your fuse even shorter with his
    support

Instead, we had to turn round, suspiciously for the bystanders!
And we stopped, only to buy from a wretched vendor
A *mudu* of auspicious fresh dates,

• **Hyladzira Balami** is a lecturer in the Department of English and Literary Studies,
  University of Maiduguri. He has a forthcoming book of poetry.

That foregrounded Mohammed Yusuf's magical dates of
    treachery
Ritual dates that bore a whiff of indoctrination
Which the Boko Haram leader fed his helots
Held captive in the sect's harrowing dungeon.

After the auspicious transaction,
The dates man pushed his wares in a wheelbarrow
Sloshing towards the ruins of the Markas, unconcerned
That the fear of Boko Haram is the beginning of wisdom!

And so that's how the Markas failed your test
Of becoming the next World Heritage Site...

But my folks are as wise as you
Who say fear prolongs life...
For you chose flight over and above fight,
Nine years clear after the event!

TANURE OJAIDE

Bypassing the Markas
(in response to Hyeladzira Balami's poem)

It wasn't fear, but flight of imaginative prescience that marked
the U-turn; it was pointless pointing at the perforated walls
that half-blind see a kilometre away from the intersection.
The spectacle of Eiffel Tower, the Twin Towers of KL, the
    Statue
celebrating liberty all tell us what needs to be seen is beauty;
    not
bloodletting by devotees of evil djinns masquerading divinity.
I see beauty and marvel at the vision of eyefuls of art; I have
lauded the ugly as beautiful in my people's moulds, figures
but will not choose fright over beauty. Let cold blood not be
the colour whose shades make Picasso and Owena Bruce
    divine!

Needless death can only fill fools but cannot triumph over life.
There's no cause marching over IEDs to boast of a charmed
    life—
it wasn't fear that caused the cry to bypass the Markas; no
    flight.
Call it fear that the lion smelt the hunter and retreated to its
    den;
call it fear that the old hunter of leopards went back for his
    charms.
Life is fearsome to those who value it and know its finitude.
Hyeladzira, who does not drive recollects farther—do you still

remember Warri when I stopped you from running into
  gunshots?
How would you not choose lush dates over caked blood
  splatters?
Who spends for dates does not deserve to walk into gory
  death!

Hyeladzira, you drove and forced the argument of detour and
  all that.
You have composed a song out of your daredevilry and driving.
Let us confess our inability to tell your story of the Markas;
we who fretted over not making a shrine of the devil's
  chicanery
saw the wisdom of not singing the same song that burnt the
  city
and because the fake emir and his footloose livery fled the city;
hence those who hid from reckless shells live and you can now
  sing.
The driver and the driven have their separate songs of the tour
that took us to the festival supper Adama prepared to charm
  us.
Imagine her waiting for her visitors and not for any bad news!
Pointless pointing over perforated houses to Ground Zero; we
  saw.

We arrived home who have seen the spectacles of distant
  lands.
How could a resident of Madagali or Sukur canonize the one
who cannibalized prehistoric civilizations and burned his
  library?

Hyeladzira, don't compare these things; they are not
    comparable:
Sukur and the Markas; magnificent heights and the savage low!
Sightseeing is a form of sport to us tourists of the land and
no-one wishes to overstretch fun to take the better side of him.
You say it was fear that set up the flight. What else drives one
from absurdities fools take for epic fight but only quizzical
    fancy?
It wasn't fear that caused the detour from the Markas spot.
It was the sweet dates, Adama's buffet, and songs of survival.

ABUBAKAR A. OTHMAN

The Site Not Seen
(For H. A. Balami)

You invited us for a tour of the torn city
Ojaide and I,
You hurried us towards the Markas,
Its bullet ridden Madras of madness beckoning,
Begging us for recognition
As World Heritage Site.

Not every ruins are relics for history
Some are debris of our follies
That sully without solace
Our collective conscience.

We cringed from the fringe
Of this heritage site of ignominy
Our protest forcing you to a detour
Bringing to a halt the tour.

We drove away not in flight
Nor for lack of the Will to fight
But a deliberate reaction to slight
This choice of heritage site.

The Curator of Markas

Our man, the curator
Relishes the stench of combusted bodies
Decomposing in the dank ashes
Of the relics of Markas.
With blood-shut eyes he drives fiendishly
Screeching tyres on charred remains
Of incombustible bones buried
In the rubbles of Markas.

His mortuary cold coffin-car
Sped us through the metropolis of Yerwa
To the bullet-ridden Necropolis of Markas.
Accustomed to Markas' dry dates of death
He denied us the delight of Yerwa's fresh dates of life
Hawked in the wheel-barrows along the serene streets of
    Maiduguri:
To him there is no better place to be
Than the dungeon of Markas
A new World Heretics Site.

The dead are not the victims of war, they are gone
But those broken but not gone,
Who have lost touch of humanity
Living on the verge of insanity,
They are like the fire-flies
Hovering around the fire of death.
They know not the difference
Between fireworks and furnace of fire,
And for our man, the curator
There's no difference between the green statue of Liberty
And the scarlet minaret of Markas.

RAZINAT T. MOHAMMED

The Three Musketeers
(Ojaide, Balami and Othman)

What a sin that you three left for the Markas without the
amazons
And with such animated delight your stories tell
The stories that neither bravery nor cowardice convey
For the missing amazons on your tails you avoid.
Do you now choose the sweetness of dry dates over healthy
    cuisine?
Could you not think that the beauty of an Amazon was more
    uplifting a sight?
Yes! The Eiffel Tower, the Twin Towers of KL and the statue
celebrating liberty are all edifying sights but would you choose
to look at mere monuments over the contours of a waiting
Amazon? What has become of you Balami that you shoo these
two to a site like Markas?
What is there to see in the Markas but the bitter history of mad
    men written in blood?
The bullet ridden walls tell only a heinous tale
And like the invaders' bullets on the ruins of the Castle of
    Byblos
They offer nothing but the memorials of whimsical actions of
    men
At a point in time in the history of human evolution to
    civilization.
Do not mock our efforts with cravings for such a savage sight
For our hearts have bled in supplications for the safe return of
    our heroes gone
On a cruise for fresh air while the tables were being laid

Unknown to us, they had made a detour for adventure or
    curiosity
None worth the sacrifice and in comparison to the tender
    palms of the Amazon.

PART III

FICTION AND NON-FICTION

My Daughter, My Blood

- *Razinat T. Mohammed*

The girl, Mariya, knelt on the sand in the small courtyard. She was on all four to support herself from the pressure of squatting on her toes. Her face covered in sweat, tears running down her young face like river tributaries finding lower plains. Her bulging stomach reaching down to her knees buried in the sand. The compound, small and untidy was dotted by cooking utensils, broken plastic wares, fire wood and other odds scattered and seeming like the occupants had recently experienced a sand storm. The house was a two bedroom simple structure built of cement blocks. A zinc batcher patched along the right side of the horizontal wall from where sounds of bleating sheep could be heard even as the stench from decayed ammonia envelop the compound. The sun was overhead and the girl, Mariya only twenty-one, was bowed in respect before her father, Adamu. He was a mason whose income was very irregular and when he did not find work as a mason, he often worked as a labourer just so that he can feed his family. He had wished that Mariya would someday complete her secondary education and perhaps, read a professional course and help the family in the future. His other children sadly, were not committed to their studies and had never been commended by teachers in their schools. And since the disappearance of his daughter, Hawa his younger daughter had remained at home for fear of falling victim to the incessant kidnapping of school girls in the State. Her mother stood clutching the door pane, her eyes red from crying. Adamu was standing over Mariya screaming menacingly at the top of his voice. There was actually no need for all the shouting because the object of his anger was right in front of him. Her frightened son, a toddler, was at a corner having been kicked by the angry man. The child was not in any mood for playing; he sat with his back to the wall and his tiny legs stretched in front of him. Although he was happy to have reached the end of their tortuous journey, he could not explain what was happening to his mother. He was happy to rest his weary feet after days of trekking. All was not well in the house, even the little boy could tell. The father, a diminutive man in his late fifties was pointing his bony fingers in the direction of the girl whose exhausted body was quivering at every word that came out of his mouth.

"I cannot tolerate having you and that child in my house, not to talk of the one you are carrying Mariya."

The tone of his voice had a finality that left both Mariya and her mother in tears. Mariya's mother, Uwani, a quiet and obedient woman who had eloped with Adamu and married him against her father's wish, had lived with her choice in spite of his ill tempers and irrational decisions. Over the years, she had watched him silently take one wrong decision after another only for him to have regrets afterwards. The decision he was taking in respect of Mariya, their first-born child was again one of those wrong decisions and she felt helpless because he had refused to listen to her pleadings. How many years have they waited for the return of their daughter? Where did they not go in search of her? How many meetings did he attend as one of the parents of the kidnapped school girls? How could he be refusing to accept her back simply because she returned with a child? Many more questions ran the rounds in her head and she could not help her poor child except cry with her.

"But father!" she raised her head up to face her father, "what am I to do and where will I go to? I escaped from the forest with great difficulty, dragging this child with me because I missed you all. Father, our lives in the forest is a very difficult one, they married me to one of their commanders and he constantly abused me and there was nothing anyone of us girls could do. Every one of us that was taken away that day, we all have children by them. What was I to do?"

Her tears were profuse.

"Why did you not wait until you have delivered the thing you are carrying before returning to me? And why did you have to drag that thing to this house? Did you not think of your father and the shame you would be bringing to him? Did you not think about your father when you where taking all of these decisions? Amongst the fifty-three girls kidnapped that day, you are the first to return and you come to me like this? What do you want me to do Mariya?"

He was emotional and broke down in tears and whatever he said afterwards came out of his mouth in fits.

"You are better off dead Mariya. Or better still, I should die rather than live with this shame you have brought to me," Adamu said without looking at the girl.

Both Mariya and her mother opened their mouths in shock.

"Dead? What are you even talking about? How can you pronounce death on your own daughter? All the meetings that you attended and the prayers for her safe return were for nothing then? How can a father wish death for his daughter and in what ways did this child go wrong? Do you think that any of the girls wanted to be kidnapped and molested forcibly by those dirty men? Do you think that a woman's body chooses whom to be pregnant for? Could she or any of the girls for that matter shut their wombs and stop it from bulging with child? How can you even think in this direction?"

"Say whatever you want Uwani. I cannot live with the shame that has visited my home. This is the simple truth. Besides, we are barely surviving, you, me and the children so how can she come with her bastard children and want me to take responsibility for them when their father is somewhere maybe making other babies with the free women at his disposal? Be reasonable Uwani, this is a matter that is beyond me. I can take her to the rehabilitation camp if she wants but not in this house."

He was perspiring profusely and wiping his tears with the sleeves of his *Jallabiya*. He had froth forming at the corners of his mouth.

Mariya's tears had stopped flowing; she was prepared for the worst. After all, she had seen and experienced rejection in the four years since her kidnapping. She was used to eating once a day and water was a luxury they had had to live without for most of the day.

"I am used to eating just once, Father. My feeding will not pose any problem to you. And this boy I can share with him whatever I get so you don't have to consider him an extra mouth, please Father. I came to live with my family please; I am begging you in the name of *Allah*. What will I do with him? I cannot throw him away, Father."

She was already crying again. She did not want to imagine throwing her child away because she was the only parent that the boy had. His father had been killed in one of the operations even before she was delivered of the child. She was remarried to another man when her son began to take his first few steps. She was in a dilemma and at that point she could only turn to look at her mother whose face was awash with tears.

"Listen to what you are saying! You have even forgotten about the one or ones you are carrying. You really need to see it from my point of view; the government has a camp where you and your children will be better off Mariya. I can take you there before neighbours know what has happened."

At that point, she realised the futility in arguing with her father on the matter. Her mind went back to the risks she took in escaping from her captors. Were all her efforts turning futile? In a flash, her mind travelled down the path that led her to that spot. She saw herself dragging the tired toddler behind her equally heavy feet. The nightmares as her body suffered under the weight of pregnancy, her son's cry for water when they had just drops left. She saw herself on the first night after her escape. Joyful for finding a cluster of shrubs and after clearing the foliage in order to spread an old sugar sack she had rolled into an old torn shopping bag she had carried for the journey. She saw her tired son close his eyes as soon as his head touched the sack; his cracked lips sore and the flies that perched on the wounds in search of moisture. She saw herself, sitting by his side as darkness enveloped them and how she could not succumb to deep sleep for fear that wild animals could come and drag her son away. She saw herself promising her son a better life with sweets and biscuits all those little things little children like to have. What did he know of sweets but all the same, she promised him such little things that she told him are the best things he could ever taste as a little child. She saw the ashes on her bare feet as she walked through deserted villages. She saw how in her fitful sleep, she had imagined her return home with excitement. And how she imagined her family would receive her with great jubilation. She did not see her father standing above her and rejecting to take her back because her body failed to device a means to stop the unwanted pregnancies.

She lifted her head and looked straight at her father and right then, a surge of emotion brought hot tears flowing down her dusty cheeks again. This was her reality. She could not wish to return to the forest and she could not do anything about her son or the unborn. She was therefore willing to accept whatever her father thought was the best in the prevailing situation. She looked towards her demoralized mother again, crunched to the threshold. Her sadness written on the page of her tear stained face. She was sure that her mother was as helpless as she was and what could they do? As women, they could not have it their way. The men did whatever they thought could serve their best interest. It was not important if the female involved shared blood affinity with them.

Adamu and the two women remained silent each to his or her own thoughts. The boy walked towards its mother as the call for prayer was heard from the neighbouring *Masjid*. Adamu was startled and muttered some inaudible words and picked a small kettle and disappeared into the open-topped latrine in the compound. Mariya did not make a move to stand up. She kept her head bowed, her stomach extended downwards even as her whimpering son clung to her right shoulder.

As she remained in her kneeling position under the hot sun, the thought of what she did wrongly besieged her mind. She cast her mind's eye again to the very beginning. In the four years of her incarceration, she had often reverted to the night of their abduction. She was in her dormitory arguing with Saudatu the girl sleeping above her bunk when they heard the sounds of approaching trucks and footsteps along the corridors. It was not quite the time for lights out and so some of the girls were haranguing at one another and others were going round the beds begging for something to snack on, *kuli-kuli*, *gari*, *kamzo* or whatever anyone could part with, while some others were playing the pillow game. It was usual for them to while away time in these manners. The booted men had shooed them into some waiting trucks and before they could tell what was happening they were heading into the neighbouring Sambisa Forest. They were not given enough time to dress properly as some were still in their uniforms since returning from their night studies. She was jolted back to the present by a male voice at the main entrance to the compound calling to her father. When she turned to the voice, the man stopped suddenly in obvious shock. His mouth hanged open for a while and when he regained his composure, her father had come out of the latrine and literarily shooed the visitor out of the compound. As they walked out together, Mariya heard the man's voice asking if the first daughter of the house had returned. But her father was silent. His silence merged into the tangible one that enveloped the house afterwards.

Mariya adjusted herself and sat on her buttocks, looked towards her mother, not sure what was going on in her mind. At that moment, Uwani walked to her daughter and they embraced even as the tears began to run down their cheeks.

"My child, I am happy that you have returned alive. Do not worry about your father's decision. We will find a way out. The

Lord and idol of my worship will not let me down when I need Him the most."

"Mama, Mama please help me. Help me make my father accept me. What is my offence in all of these?" she begged in a voice that betrayed her uncertainties. She was exhausted first from the long trek and then the prolonged sadness caused by her father's unexpected treatment. The little boy was clung to her shoulders and his whimpering voice was rising when they heard the returning footsteps of the men. Mariya made the boy sit down in front of her. Uwani quietly returned to her former position before their neighbour, Mallam Hassan walked into the compound with her husband.

"*Mariya, sannu, sannu Mama na,*"* Hassan spoke in Hausa. He was overwhelmed by sympathy for the girl. From the way he ran towards her, Mariya was sure he had been told the whole story. He robbed the toddler's head and the child clung to his mother the more.

"Adamu, this is a happy day. We need to inform the chairman of the Parents' Association of this new development. May Allah be praised!"

He was carrying on with his excitement while Adamu's contorted face tightened the more. He was angry at Mallam Hassan for even suggesting telling the whole community about the shameful thing that had befallen him. How is he going to face the community when everyone learns that his daughter has returned, not alone but with a child and not just that, with another due in weeks? He felt like evaporating into thin air or even screaming in protest and yet, he could neither perform the disappearing act nor open his mouth wide to scream before

---

* Consoling greeting

them all. As he felt his blood boil inside his veins, he could not control himself and he shouted at the ranting man to stop immediately.

"What nonsense are you talking about now? Is she your child that you are making plans of what to do and who to tell?"

Mallam Hassan stopped abruptly, his half opened mouth hanging. He did not believe his ears at first. He looked from the man talking to the wife standing dejectedly by the door and to the girl, Mariya, crunched on the sand and finally to the runny nosed toddler still holding on to his mother's *Himar*. He could not understand why Adamu who had always been in the fore-front at parents' meetings and during their meetings with government representatives and non-governmental organizations would not want to inform the community.

"My dear brother, please, in the name of *Allah*, do not push this line of thought. We all have been praying for the safe return of our children and now yours has risked her life and returned to you and you are trying to delay sending the cheery news to the community? What kind of behaviour is this?"

Hassan was suspicious of his friend.

"I don't want the community to know of her return, not just yet."

"But why, why my dear friend?" an exasperated and sad Hassan demanded.

"I can accept my daughter but not with those unwanted children she has returned with. Mallam Hassan, what is difficult for you to understand here? My daughter is my blood but not some evil blood that may turn out a murderer in the future. Do you know the meaning of *blood*? Will you like your own blood to be diluted with these evil people? Why do you want mine to be so polluted?"

He was beginning to hub from one point to another in the attempt to stress his point.

"Are you trying to tell me that you don't want your daughter anymore?"

"I want my daughter Hassan. It is these children of evil men that I do not want in my house."

At this point, Adamu was again foaming in the mouth as his arms kept swaying and pointing towards Hassan's face.

"Yes, I understand your point. What do you say about your daughter's own position then? Is the child not her own son? Or is the one she is carrying not a part of her? How do you think she will disown her own children? Like you, she sees them as her own flesh and blood. Please be reasonable, my friend."

"Pray for your daughter to return with children by those evil men and I will like to see how easily you embrace them into your home. You know what these people are like and you are the one telling me to accept one or two of them into my family, *habawa*...?" hissing and turning his face in disgust.

"Please Mallam Hassan help me make him see reason. How can we throw away our first-born child? Is it her fault that she is with child and had borne another? Was it by choice that she followed the men who kidnapped her? Did we not send our daughter to school like every parent in this town? Where did this child go wrong please Mallam Hassan? Help me make him accept this child as she is. I am a mother who has suffered the loss of a child and when *Allah* returns the same child to me, someone is telling me to refuse to accept her? No please my husband, you cannot send our child back to her tormentors."

Uwani was on the floor scratching and tearing at her hair. Mariya and her toddler were also crying from where they squatted. Mallam Hassan did not know what to do. He walked to his friend and placing a hand on his shoulder whispered tenderly into his ears.

"I said it will not happen."

Adamu's reaction was sudden and Hassan was startled and jumped backwards.

"And I warn you not to bring anyone into this matter. It is my family problem and as the head of this family, I will solve the problem in the way and manner I deem fit. I thank you for coming but please and please do not have any part in this matter beyond this," raising both hands up as though he was in prayer.

Mallam Hassan saw the move as a dismissal and said his apologies and with his head downcast, walked out of the narrow gate. At that very moment, Uwani gave a loud outcry and as if embolden by the submission of the man, Hassan, she walked to her husband and charged at him like a wounded cat.

"You will not carry out this vicious threat while I am alive. If this girl leaves this house then I promise you that I will leave too. I cannot continue to stay and watch you destroy my life and those of my children without a word. You have done enough Mallam Adamu. Stand up Mariya and carry your child with you. You will not return to the forest and you will not poison your children because your father wishes for that. Even though they are offsprings of those evil people, upbringing shall change their destinies. We will not die, let us go."

Adamu was opened-mouthed for the most part of what he thought was Uwani's charades. But when he saw the woman enter her room and emerged with a little bundle under her armpit, he walked towards her as if to stop her but restrained himself. Uwani helped Mariya up and held the little toddler by hand and walked towards the gate.

"Uwani, do not return to this house after this behaviour," they heard Adamu's voice announce. But rather than feel regrets, Uwani held her head up and straight as she led the way, not sure what lay ahead in their world of uncertainties.

Command and Compliance

- *Abubakar A. Othman*

Zzzhi-zzzhu, zzzhi-zzzhu came the jazzy tune on his cell-phone. He picked the call immediately and answered with a greeting, "Hello!"

Then the caller responded accordingly, "Hello", and continued without stating who he was, "am I speaking with the Head of the Department of Languages and Linguistics?", he asked without the courtesy of adding the word 'please' that civilized speakers are wont to do.

"Yes, you are speaking with the Head, Professor Dauda Lamba. Who am I speaking with, please?" he replied the man in the manner of the educated and civilized.

"Good," said the man and went on now to introduce himself more out of intimidation than want of intimacy. 'My name is Major-General Donald Langtang, speaking from the Defence Headquarters, Ajuba.'

Silence.

Deep, visible, palpable silence.

In the brief but loud silence Professor Dauda Lamba seemed to have gone six feet under, but for the rise and fall motion of his chest. His eyes were wide open with the eyeballs starring fixedly into space. His mouth hung out like someone who has crushed hot pepper in the soup he is eating. Sitting petrified, leaning languidly on the left arm of the swivel chair, his right hand holding the cell-phone to his ear, motionless, Prof. Lamba, indeed, appeared to be dead in that condition. And who wouldn't in the circumstance?

It was in the heat of the Jihadists atrocities in the Sahel region of Bargu Caliphate. The region's capital city of Irugudiam, now renamed Darul Islam by the Jihadists, and was experiencing rampant incidents of killings, abduction and hostage-taking of politically exposed persons and intellectuals. The city's only university, the University of Bargu, was the worst-hit with the regular abduction and killing of lecturers and kidnapping of students. Prof. Lamba's neighbour was the latest victim of abduction on the campus and he knew the psychological trauma the family went through while his release was being negotiated for five million naira which the family could not afford.

The abductors were law onto themselves. They usually operate in the dead of the night; they came dressed in full military uniform and driving military vehicles. The Command and Control unit of the military in Bargu has always denied military involvement in the crime, claiming that they were being impersonated. But if the abductors were impersonators were they also invisible or untouchable? The city was under dusk-to-dawn curfew, how then some people could drive through the barricaded and heavily guarded streets of the city late at night without detection? Where were the soldiers at the numerous stop-and-check points? Where were the Joint Task Force Patrol teams always cockroaching through the empty streets in the silent night? How could these miscreants defy all those checks and controls and drive freely in the city, breaking into shops and houses, looting and abducting people without being apprehended. Indeed, as the Hausa saying goes, *biriya kama da mutum.*[*]

---

[*] Literally, "A monkey looks much like Man." ...situations or circumstances that are likely to be true.

The miscreants were also daring in their activities; they do not take their victims by surprise but with derring-do. They first of all send you a letter informing you of their coming and stating what you must do to save your life. Then a tart reminder follows, warning you if you tarry in your response. But when it got to the point of making a phone call to you, then your time is up but for few hours. For Prof. Lamba the phone call was even from a Major-General; it did not matter whether the call was from the Defence Headquarters in Ajuba or from Ground Zero in the Sahel desert of Borgu, they all use the same uniforms and weapons.

"Hello! Are you there Prof.?" came the hoarse voice again to jolt him back to life.

"Yes sir. What can I do for you sir?" replied Prof. Lamba, his voice was fricative with fear.

"Prof. I need your assistance, please," the hoarse voice was now calm and decorous. "My son has just finished his studies in your department but cannot graduate because he has a pending course that I understand to be yours. I have already secured a place for him at the National Defence Academy and a team will be visiting your University for background check on him as is the tradition of integrity with the military. If it is found out that he is yet to graduate because of one course, he will be thrown out of the Academy and that will not be good for me as a Major-General."

Professor Lamba took a deep breath of relief and relaxed properly in his chair before responding to the Major-General. And when he did he spoke with the charisma of a Professor and with air of authority as a Head of Department.

"Well, Major-General! I cannot tell you anything now until I check the records to confirm the academic status of your son, if you would give me his full name, please."

Patrick Donald Langtang was among the fifty-eight students that recently completed their studies for a Bachelors of Arts degree in Languages and Linguistics. However, seven of them were to spend an additional semester of the next academic year to re-sit their examinations in the courses they failed. Some have two or more courses against their names but Patrick was lucky to have only one. Professor Lamba immediately got back to the Major-General to explain to him the situation.

"Hello, sir," answered the Major-General as he picked the call.

"Good afternoon, Major…" began the Prof. but he was interrupted immediately by him with a correction.

"Major-General please, not Major," forgetting momentarily the self-imposed politeness he started with.

"Major-General Sir," said Prof., "I called to confirm to you that your son Patrick has failed in LLH435: Hausa Syntax. However, the course was taught by Professor Garba Dankabo who is a senior colleague in the department…"

Again the Major-General interrupted him, this time even impudently.

"Listen to me my friend! You are the Head of Department and a Professor. There is nobody senior to you in your department. Direct that so-called senior colleague of yours to remark my son's script and pass him. It is a matter of chain of command and compliance. Hope I made myself clear, Mr. Professor?"

"Yes, sir. I understand you. Unfortunately, this type of command and compliance works only in the military but not in the academia. Here in the University we are guided by truth, honesty and moral rectitude."

"Professor Rectitude, I've no time for platitude, be blunt, tell me what is your price?"

"Major-General sir, my price is my conscience and no amount of money can buy it."

"My dear Professor, I hope you remember the status of the officer you are talking to?"

"Is that a threat sir?"

"No, it is a reminder to you that you are talking to a Major-General in the army."

"That is the rank of a Reader in the University, in case you don't know Mr. Major-General. I am a fully-fledged Professor, a rank higher than that of a General in the army."

Meanwhile, the Major-General's wife was within earshot and could hear the outburst of her husband. She sounded more intelligent and better informed than her husband, as is the case with most of these army officers and their wives. She was aware that most lecturers in the University pride themselves for high moral standard. But that was then in her days as a young undergraduate, she was not sure if it is still the case today. These days she has seen instances where Professors in the corridors of power conduct themselves in the most despicable manners. She has seen several of them being kicked around by barely literate politicians who they serve as Special Advisers, Special Assistants, Protocol Officers or Speech Writers. Therefore, the issue of conscience is at best an opinion but certainly not fact. Professor Lamba may be different but he cannot speak for all Professors in the university.

"My dear, you don't shout on phone to a person you have not met before," the wife cautioned her insolent husband, "and besides you are the one asking for a favour from him. You ought to be polite and diplomatic."

"These bloody civilians must be talked to that way to make them understand that *khaki no bi leda*," retorted the man.

"He is not a bloody civilian my dear, he is a Professor and Head of Department in the university," the wife explained to her husband, and then added jokingly, "of course, *khaki no bi leda* and University no bi *mami*; learn to speak their language."

She then took the phone from her husband and copied into her own the telephone number of Professor Dauda Lamba, just in case she might need to get across to him herself.

Professor Lamba now found himself in a quandary over his situation. This was the third month they have been without salary and the city has been under a dire economic crunch consequent upon the insecurity situation. There are no shops as usual where he can buy foodstuff on credit, the owners of the very few ones around, are reluctant to sell on credit being uncertain if the creditor will live to see the next day. What with the rampant disappearance and abduction of staff on the campus, nobody will trade in debt with potentially dead people. Prof. Lamba needed money desperately to save his family from starvation but his conscience will not allow him get it just from anybody.

What's your price?, he recalled the Major-General's impudent question with chagrin. *What effrontery? Couldn't he have put it more decently, something like an indirect offer, Prof. life must be hard for you these days without salary, how are you coping? Good! At least there is some empathy here. Prof. would you accept some little assistance, please? Better!* A very polite offer. *I hope he calls back to apologize and ameliorate me with a polite offer and request.*

As he soliloquized over his quandary his cell-phone rang, he quickly answered the call without finding out first who the caller was.

"Hello! Major-General," but a female voice answered him instead, "Hello Prof., my name is Salamatu Langtang, wife to Major-General Donald Langtang. How are you doing sir?"

"I'm doing fine, Madam. I've just spoken with your husband. He was not fair to me I must say."

"Prof. I sincerely apologize on his behalf. I heard everything and I must admit my husband was very wrong in his approach."

"How may I help you Madam," he initiated the request himself having found a more refined person to talk with, instead of the uncouth soldier. But he was soon to discover that bad manners are a family disease in the military.

"I'd rather offer to help you first Prof. You've been without salary for months. May I have your bank account number, please?"

"Not to worry Madam, I can cope, I'm coping."

"I'm not trying to bribe you to help my son. I'm only sympathizing with you as a family man without salary. Don't try to play tough and lose out please?"

"Lose out Madam, what do you mean?"

"Don't forget that the course is not yours and the owner is your senior colleague, chain of command and compliance applies here as well."

"So does check and balance, Madam. The bucks end here on my table!"

"Not entirely, Prof."

"Says who, Madam?"

"Prof. do not interrogate me, I'm a product of the university system if you must know."

"Then you and your husband can do your worst if you think the University is an extension of the military barracks."

"Thank you, Prof. for the insults. My husband will definitely get back to you," and she disconnected the call.

As the phone went dead in his ear, a fresh fear immediately gripped him.

He began to blame himself for talking without restraint. He wanted a polite offer and here was a more considerate woman who wanted to do so but he allowed his ego to override his sense of rational judgment. The fact that he contemplated accepting the offer made him culpable, and now that he had bungled it he made himself a potential soft target for the next victim of abduction, or so he thought.

I'm sure my abduction will come soon. The woman has threatened that her husband will get back to me, which means that her husband will get at me, and when that happens it will be without any demand for ransom. They know I have nothing but my conscience and the word is an anathema to them.

As the apprehension for abduction dawned heavily on him he resigned to his fate and braced up for the occasion, quoting Shakespeare for fortitude, "cowards die many times before their death, the valiant never tastes of death but once. Upon all the wonders I yet have heard it seems to me most strange that men should fear death knowing that death a necessary end will come when it will come."

Prof. Lamba was in the office throughout that day, and he was virtually the only person left in the department at 4:00pm.

Since the upsurge of killings and abduction on the campus, the staff closed from work as early as 2:00pm. Lecture hours were slashed by half for each course, while for the whole day it took just five hours instead of the normal ten or twelve hours as the case may be. On some days lectures hardly took place, as the Jihadists often attacked the University environs, sending shivers and fears into the campus.

Unfortunately for Prof. Lamba that day happened to be one such day. At about 4pm while he was busy preparing results for Senate meeting the next day, an attack was launched on the military barrack close to the University. The attack happened in such a mind-boggling manner that left most people wondering if it was not the military attacking itself. There seemed be two factions of the military in the crisis, with a third force made up of the military High Command. While one faction was genuinely committed to fighting and defeating the Jihadists, the other faction seemed to be enjoying the crisis and would not want to see its end. Hence, each time a significant achievement appeared to have been made against the Jihadists, a tactical error of logistics will occur and segments or detachments of the army will be overrun and their arms and ammunitions seized by the Jihadists.

The attackers came in a convoy of motorbikes carrying AK47 riffles, machetes, cudgels and all manner of crude weapons. They made a bridge of sand across the deep trench that surrounded the barracks and crossed over into the barracks, with very minimal resistance from the soldiers on duty. The attackers went straight to the armoury and broke it open and carted away all the arms and ammunitions kept inside. They also broke open the military cell and let out over a thousand of their members detained inside the cell.

Well after the attackers had left, a lazy military aircraft appeared in the horizon irritating the already devastated civilian population of the city with the burring sound of its engine, hovering over the city in idle reconnaissance. Prof. Lamba called his house to assure his family of his safety and to warn the children against loitering outside while the reconnaissance lasted.

The campus went dead silent with neither vehicle nor human movement outside. Students remained huddled up in their hostels while the staff remained indoors in their houses or trapped in their offices. Prof. Lamba was trapped in his office as he was busy throughout the day working on students' status. But now the relative peace of the environment has been disturbed and he could no longer work with concentration. He brought down the window blinds to shield him from the light outside and turned on the door lock for security while he remained cocooned inside. Suddenly his cell-phone rang. It startled him with the fear that it may be from the Major-General, or his boys, perhaps to tell him that the incident that just happened at the barracks may as well affect him as a collateral victim.

The attack was not on the University of course, but it was too close for comfort. With people running helter-skelter, it was possible too that the miscreants could have infiltrated the campus to abduct him. He did not pick the call for fear of the unknown; he did not even care to find out who made the call. Then the call came a second time and a third in successive order. He remained indifferent nevertheless, forcing himself instead to concentrate on the files in front of him. Then came a message tone; it was safer for him to read a text message than to respond to a call where the fear and trepidation of his voice will expose his weakness. The text was from the Vice-Chancellor: *Prof. Lamba your attention is needed immediately in my office.* Brief like a threat or a warrant of arrest.

It was almost 6:00pm and time for the *Magrib* prayers, but these days very few people went to the mosque. With the rampant attacks and incidents of suicide bombings in the mosques, people prayed in their homes and offices and hurriedly barricaded their gates before curfew time at 7:00pm. He performed the *Magrib* prayers alone in his office and rushed out to the Senate Building which was a walking distance from his office. At the Senate Building there were no people around, only the university security men and the soldiers assigned to guard the place. He walked passed them without greeting anybody, no one daring to stop him just as he was also oblivious of them. To him everybody was a suspect in this crisis and the so-called security men and the military were no less obvious. He took the lift to the 7th floor and went straight to the V.C's office.

"I've an urgent call from the V.C. a while ago," he told the V.C.'s secretary rather audaciously.

"I'm aware of that, the door is open," replied the V.C.'s secretary equally sententiously.

The V.C. was with some principal officers of the university and few others who were not members of the university community. Among them was a female military officer in uniform whom he recognized as his student years back.

"Good evening sir," he greeted the Vice Chancellor, ignoring the others as a matter of protocol.

"Have a seat," ordered the V.C. as if it were a way of answering his greeting. Then he added, "Prof. Lamba, sorry we had to call you out at this inauspicious time. As you can see we are on top of the security situation. I called you for a different matter though. This young lady officer was actually our student, I hope you recognize her."

"Yes I do," replied Prof. Lamba sharply and went on to greet her by way of welcome, "welcome Miss Debbie Dan."

"Major Debbie Dan, if you don't mind sir," she corrected him politely.

Prof. Lamba smiled knowingly, cursing the soldiers beneath his smile for being sticklers with ranks.

"Now that you know each other," continued the V.C, "I'm sure you are in a better position to solve her problem. She came with a message from the Defence Headquarters and she is under instruction not to make an unprofitable return," explained the Vice Chancellor who then asked Major Debbie to go with Prof. Lamba into the Committee Room next door and discuss the problem.

"Debbie, what the hell is going on?" asked Prof. Lamba as soon as they entered into the Committee Room.

"Sorry I had to correct you before the V.C. It was dictated by officialdom, now you can address me the way you used to, Debbie Baby!"

They both looked at each other longingly, smiling as they hugged themselves.

"When did you join the army to rise to the rank of a Major?" he asked as soon as they sat down.

"I was already a Senior Intelligence Officer when I came in as a student. I did so well reporting on the university that immediately after my graduation I was promoted to the rank of a Major," Debbie explained.

"A Major and very soon a Major-General, not for fighting and wining battles but for eavesdropping, gossiping and stealing university secrets for your Boss!" retorted Prof. Lamba

"Call it what you may but you must give me credit for being a loyal girlfriend to you. I would have recorded all our bedroom talks and office chats and used that to nail you, but I placed love above service. Well, every good turn deserves another; my boss needs your help and knowing my relationship with you he has asked me to fly in immediately to get it done. The military jet hovering in the air right now has nothing to do with the fracas awhile ago at the barracks; it was the jet that flew me in from Ajuba. I understand you took a hard position on his request and even turned down his attempt to bribe you. I faulted him on that stressing on your quality of self-pride and strength of character, but couldn't tell him your only weakness," she explained her mission wrapped in retrospective facts.

"Then how did he discover the weakness and sent you back to me? I guess you are also his mistress?" Prof. Lamba responded to her insinuation with equal accusation.

"You and your jealousy…you've hardly changed!"

After discussing Major Debbie's request and resolving the issue amicably, Prof. Lamba revisited her earlier statement relating to the attack on the military barracks.

"Did you call that attack on the barracks a mere fracas, Major Debbie?"

"Point of correction! 'Debbie darling, not Major Debbie'." As long as the jet is hovering in the sky and Debbie is hibernating here in the room with you, she remains Debbie Darling for old times' sake," she explained jovially with longing in her eyes.

"Not in this room anyway, perhaps in the other room," he responded, equally jokingly and longingly.

Home is no place to Stay

- Safiya Ismaila Yero

Alhaji Saleh sat up in bed for the third time. He listened to the rising and falling of his wife's breathing as she slept on beside him the eight spring mattress, having locked out the agony of a mother whose child had been kidnapped by the Boko Haram sect for a little over two years. He wished he could do the same too- allow sleep wrap him in a blanket of peace and take him on a journey back in time when all was well, when his daughter was alive and safe; when his company along University Road in Maiduguri had not been raided and razed to the ground by the same people who kidnapped his daughter and slaughtered his best friend like a Sallah Ram. His wife stirred and mumbled something inaudible. He wasn't sure where her dreams led her- to the laughter that once filled their home or to the deafening sound of guns and cries of pain and blood stench and biting hunger. The pain stabbed at his heart again. He thought of waking her up to tell her about the invisible needle that pierced his heart anytime Ameerah visited his thoughts, or his dreams. Tonight, she was neither in his thoughts nor in his dreams – she was there in the room. Little wonder that the needle that pierced his chest was substituted with an arrow- she was close, he knew it. He stretched his hands in the darkness and groped, expecting to get hold of the fabric of her china white *hijab*, the one she was wearing the last time he saw her.

He winced as the pain hit him like a wave, squeezing his heart. She was here. He listened, but the only sounds he heard were the steady breathing of Ahmad and Goni, and the laboured breathing of Fantah, who had been battling with blocked nostrils since three days now.

Alhaji Saleh stood up and headed for the door, careful not to step on any of his five children huddled together on the floor, fast asleep.

The room was the size of his bathroom, back in Maiduguri. Made from tarpaulin, the room had no windows, so the opening covered with a worn out curtain doubled as a door and window.

He drew the curtain and held it back with a rope to let in air, and invariably, mosquitoes. Alhaji Saleh hated mosquitoes, but it was better to be bitten by mosquitoes and have malaria than to be suffocated or risk his children contracting some illness because of the lack of air. So he had learnt to put up with them, just as he had learnt to make do with a lot of things which, under normal circumstances, he did not put up with. But this was not a normal circumstance. He knew that they all should not be crammed in a room half the size of a market stall. It was difficult to believe that two years after they escaped from their Boko- Haram infested home, they were still living in such doleful situation, still praying that the Boko Haram insurgents will be eliminated by the Nigerian Army and they would all return to Borno, or what would be left of it.

Two years on, and the Army was still battling to wipe the insurgents.

And he still managed to feed his children.

He would sit under the huge mango tree with other men in the Internally Displaced Persons Camp in Kuchigoro, a suburb of the Federal Capital Territory, and wait for relief materials from benevolent individuals and non- governmental organizations.

And he still recounted the good old days when he gave out orders in his bread factory; when the destitute squatted and thanked him for paying their children's school fees, or wives' hospital bill.

The cool breeze outside was a welcome relief from the unbearable heat in the room. The wind caressed his face as he sat on the huge log outside his room. A mosquito whispered in his left ear and waltzed away before he could slap it. He stared with rapt attention into the dark night.

The irritable incessant chirping of a cricket peeved his ears just as the squeezing feeling in his heart became more intense.

He had tried his best to protect her. He recalled travelling to Government Girls' College Potiskum, where Ameerah was a boarding student in SS1and requested to take her home.

He did not want to take chances with the insurgents' threat of attacking secular schools.

The principal had laughed at him for taking the bluff of the Islamic sect seriously.

He had reminded her that they had already attacked police stations. She had assured him of his daughter's safety in the school and explained that schools were not the same as police stations. With a wave of the hand, she had dismissed his fears. He had taken his daughter home.

The insurgents had invaded the school soon after that. They had destroyed their facilities and burnt the place down. He was vindicated, although sad.

He realized that what they were dealing with was more ruthless than a religious group when they killed fifty boys in a

Boys' Secondary School in Buni Yadi and abducted almost three hundred girls in Government Secondary School, Chibok.

The day they attacked his mother's home, they had forcibly taken Ameerah from the house after paying a bride price of two thousand naira to his mother, who had refused to take part in the wicked game. Ameerah could not bear to see the foul smelling boys in khaki uniforms poking at her grandmother with their guns. She would never let them take her grandmother's life in her presence. For all she knew, they might kill her grandmother and still take her afterwards. Her grandmother was shouting at them, calling them names.

"Mama, I warn you to shut up for the last time. Aren't you even happy for her, that she would be married to a man serving God, and not one of these *dagutu* men of yours?"

His Kanuri accent was heavy when he said *dagutu*.

"You come in the name of religion and kill your fellow Muslims? And you have the nerve to call our good men idol worshippers? On what grounds? You say you are against Western education, yet you use phones and guns and cars. Who made all these things? Where are they imported from? You are just plain stupid. It's like saying you don't eat faeces but you eat pigs that feed on faeces. That is what you are doing, you senseless fool!"

One of them hit her on the head with the butt of his gun. He wanted to hit her again but one, who had not spoken since their arrival, stopped him. He seemed to be the leader of the group.

"Our assignment is to bring the girls. Our instruction is not to touch the older women. And the girl must come with us, willingly."

His accent was different. He did not sound like he was from Borno, or Yobe or Adamawa. He could not speak the Hausa language well. His accent reminded Ameerah of Papa Obioma, the man who sold palm oil in Gwoza market, who had mysteriously disappeared a few weeks before Gwoza was attacked. She was using a piece of cloth to stop the bleeding from the gash on her grandmother's temple.

"One more blow and she will be dead, trust me. So make your choice. Either come with us or watch her die," the third one with the Fulani accent had said.

Her grandmother had cried as Ameerah entered the tricycle the armed boys had brought. As it drove out of the compound, she heard her grandmother howling like a wounded wolf.

* * * *

It has been two years and there was no news of Ameerah. Was she dead? He could not know and the thought of not knowing was painful in itself. She was his first-born child and at birth, looked exactly like his beloved, mother. So he had named her Amina, after his mother. Ameerah became her pet name because they could not call his mother's name out of respect and tradition. He loved Ameerah so much that whenever there was news that a female suicide bomber has detonated a bomb anywhere, Alhaji Saleh always wondered if it was his beloved Ameerah. That was the pain of not knowing: you thought of anything and everything. He hated himself for not being there to protect her when she was taken. The truth was that he could not have been there, since he was forced to go into hiding when the insurgents attacked Gwoza, his beloved once peaceful town.

Alhaji Saleh could never forget the day they attacked. He had just returned from his bakery when his friend, Ba'ana, arrived. The house was empty, as his wife and children had gone to the family house to attend a naming ceremony. They were in the middle of a discussion when two young men barged into the room, panting.

"They d-d-d- they are here! They are shooting at men, and if they get hold of you, they put you in a truck, if you resist they slaughter you like a ram!" one of them said, half whispering.

He was panting. The other, a younger looking chap, was shaking as if he had just bathed with a bucket of ice on a harmattan morning. He did not speak, but his lips were moving earnestly in prayer, interjected by sobs.

Alhaji Saleh quickly locked the front door and shut all the windows. They sat quietly and waited. Each praying in his heart and hoping that it was not as bad as the boys had described. Saleh thought of his mother, his wife, children and his sister whose naming ceremony they had gone to attend. There was no way he could reach them. The GSM network in Gwoza was as good as not having one. They had to climb the rocks for suitable elevation or height in search of reception, popularly known as "network", whenever there was need for them to make phone calls.

Alhaji Saleh looked at the clock on his phone and was surprised to see that they had been seated on the same spot for over an hour. They heard gunshots, which went on for a while, and gradually faded, indicating that the gun men were heading elsewhere. When everywhere seemed quiet, Saleh told Ba'ana and the boys to wait while he surveyed the surroundings, to see if it was safe enough for them to leave for their various homes. Saleh prayed silently as he unlocked the door. His heart was pounding so hard he feared his companions would hear it, so he stepped outside brusquely, expecting a bullet or a firm grip on his ankle. He inhaled deeply when nothing of the sort happened. It was almost difficult to believe what the boys had said earlier. Everywhere seemed normal. Nothing seemed out of place, except the absence of people on the streets. But for the gunshots, he would not have believed anything had gone wrong. Sometimes, they exchanged gunfire with the police, or the Army. And sometimes they just shot in surrounding bushes in the dead of night, to remind the people of their presence. This sudden killing was alien. He remembered when they first came. They were merely preachers. Initially, there was nothing wrong with their preaching. They just preached the normal doctrines of Islam. So no one thought they were harmful, until they started preaching against secular schools, against anything Western. Saleh was confident that all was well. He went round the house to the backyard. But he still had to make sure that there was no one lurking in his backyard. He found only a malnourished cat rummaging a rubbish bin. The cat belonged to his neighbour. He headed for *Malam* Mamman's house to check on them and probably get more information about the day's events. His *salaam* was answered as he turned to leave, having salaamed thrice without any response. It was *Malam* Mamman's wife.

"Come in."

Alhaji Saleh hesitated. He knew that it was against the teachings of Islam for one to enter a married woman's house in the absence of her husband, if he was not permitted to do so. Except if there was an emergency.

"Where is *Malam*?" he asked, making no move to enter the house.

"He is inside. He asked me to tell you to come in, quickly."

She was half whispering.

Alhaji Saleh wondered why she spoke as if someone was holding a knife to her throat. He quickly stepped into the dimly lit room. She led the way into an adjoining room. *Malam* Mamman had been his neighbour for over a decade, but he had never seen the inside of his house until that day. They often met and chatted in the *masjid* after *subhi* or *magrib* prayers. In the holy month of Ramadan, they usually spread mats on their verandas and broke their fasts together, alternating between the two houses.

His eyes got accustomed to the half-lit room. It was almost seven in the evening. He would see *Malam* Mamman quickly and then go back to Ba'ana and the boys to tell them it was okay for them to go home. There were six people in the room: two grown men and four teenage boys. The man sitting next to *Malam* Mamman was sobbing like a baby.

"They killed his son," *Malam* Mamman explained, on seeing the puzzled expression on Alhaji Saleh's face.

"*Subhaanallah*! So the killings are true! There are two boys in my house now, who told me about it, but I thought they exaggerated out of fear."

"I knew it! I knew it would come to this. Since the soldiers killed their *Waziri*, I knew that we had kissed peace goodbye." The sobbing man whimpered like a wounded dog, and blew his nose noisily, collecting the mucus with the edge of his kaftan.

"The soldiers did what they had to do. The man was carrying a sack filled with ammunition which he claimed was a sack of seedlings for planting," *Malam* Mamman explained.

"Even at that, they should have just locked him up somewhere when he told them that he was the *Waziri* for Boko Haram instead of killing him."

"If they had done that, you would have been the first person to call them cowards. In fact, some of us would have accused them of working together with the insurgents if they had let that man live," Alhaji Saleh added and quickly said goodbye and turned to leave. He was already at the door when he heard sounds of approaching motorcycles and tricycles, accompanied by gunshots. He immediately retraced his steps and joined Mallam Mamman and the others.

"Please I beg for your forgiveness, Alhaji Saleh. If, as a neighbour, I offended you in anyway, do forgive me please. I know that today is my last day on earth. They are coming for us. I won't run anywhere. I am a sick man; I don't have the energy to run," said the crying man.

The boys joined in the crying.

Alhaji Saleh was irritated. He scanned the room earnestly, trying to figure out where they could hide.

"Please keep quiet," he said, wearily. Then Mallam Mamman's wife entered the room and studied the men. She decided to talk with Alhaji Saleh because he seemed to be the only one who had not fallen apart among them.

"They are coming, Alhaji."

"I know, Maman Abu, I know."

"They will kill all of you if they find you here. Please save me the trauma of witnessing that. You must hide, or find a way to move to the rocks."

She was calm, unlike the men.

Alhaji Saleh said nothing and kept examining the house. Then he heard the sounds of the motorcycles outside. Then voices he heard Ba'ana's raised voice, followed by gunshots. He closed his eyes and prayed for his friend, and felt the warmth of the tears against his cheeks. Then he heard the shots. He looked up and saw the opening in the ceiling. Maman Abu helped him with the chair and the mortar, and they all climbed into the ceiling. They heard voices in the compound shortly after the last person disappeared into the ceiling.

"*Ke! Ina maza a gidannan?*" one of them snarled at Maman Abu, demanding she shows them where the men were hiding in the house. It was the voice of a boy, a teenager perhaps. Maman Abu told them there were no men in the house, but they did not believe her, so they entered the house and started searching.

"Where is your unbeliever husband?"

"It's been two days since I last saw him," she lied.

"Well, better make up your mind that hence forth you will become our wife. Your husband is an unbeliever. We will save you by marrying you," he spat out, while the rest searched the house.

Maman Abu could not stand the ominous stench that reeked from their bodies. They checked the rooms and toilet. They even checked the water drums. By the time they were done, the house was in chaos - chairs were upturned, papers, clothes and cutlery were scattered all around. When they were satisfied that no one was hiding in the rooms, they left, after promising to come back for Maman Abu.

Alhaji Saleh and the others remained in the ceiling as the insurgents continued their 'join or die' campaign.

The ceiling was dark and filled with spiders and cobwebs. A spider crawled across Alhaji Saleh's lips. He hated spiders. It was a huge effort for him not to scream or move. They had to keep still, lest the insurgents discover their hiding place. They did not touch the women, and the very old men, and little children.

The ceiling was very uncomfortable, as they could not sit up in it, nor could they stand. Their eyes got accustomed to the darkness as the days passed. When the sun was up, the heat in the ceiling became too intense for them to bear, but they preferred it to risking their lives by coming down. They got used to the rodents that roam the ceiling at night. Their arms and feet became numb. But it was still better than dying in the hands of those bloodthirsty savages. Maman Abu used to pass water to them in plastic buckets in the dead of night, and another bucket to collect their urine and excrement. They seldom ate, except for *ruwan kanzo*, which Mama Abu passed to them. She could not risk preparing food in a large pot, because that would attract their attention, since they knew that she was alone in the house. And they always patrolled the house, as if they suspected that the men were hiding in the house. So she cooked little *tuwo*, then let it burn. She would then pour water on the burnt *tuwo* and let it soak until night, when she would strain it and pass it through the opening, to her husband and the rest, who took turns in sipping. It gave them a little energy and kept them alive. For the nine days they lived in the ceiling that was their food. They had neither prayed nor bathed nor washed their private parts after peeing. The odours from their bodies spoilt whatever good air they had. But they were alive, and that was what mattered. On the 8th day when Mama Abu visited, she explained to them that it was no longer safe for them to remain in the ceiling, that she had made arrangements for them to leave the following day. She said she would flee too, since she got news that her children, who had followed Alhaji Saleh's family to the naming ceremony, had escaped with them to Madagali, in Adamawa state.

The following day after *isha'i* prayers, Maman Abu and her sister-in- law, escorted a group of seven women in long flowing *hijabs* to the outskirts of town. They met a few Boko Haram members in soldier uniforms, their guns, slung to their necks. But because Maman Abu had engaged her sister-in-law in a chatter as they walked, the insurgents never suspected that the 'tall women' in flowing *hijabs* were actually men, so they didn't pay any attention to them. Maman Abu had provided wrappers and *hijabs* for the men, after they had shaven the hair on their faces. Mallam Mamman was not happy to part with his three-inch beard. The two women escorted the *hijabbed* men to the foot of the mountains, and then returned to Madagali, hopeful.

* * * *

Someone coughed inside the room. It must be Fantah. Tomorrow, he would take her to the IDP Clinic, he resolved. He was just about to get back inside to get some sleep when he saw the flash of her white *hijab* cut through the darkness. His heartbeat raced just as the arrows struck at his heart without mercy.

He strained his eyes, begging the darkness to retreat and let him see her, till the muscles of his eyes twitch. Drained from the effort and disappointed that she chose to play hide-and-seek with him, he closed his eyes and made to lean against the tarpaulin wall of his room, then remembered just in time that it was not concrete and dropped his head on his chest instead. His heart surged with relief when he felt her sit next to him.

Inasmuch as he wanted to hold her and look into her eyes, he dared not open his eyes, for fear that she might flee. He could hear her breathing. Her thigh was next to his and their shoulders brushed.

"I dreamt about her."

His eyes flew open as disappointment replaced relief. He could not understand why he didn't hear her footsteps as she left the room. He wanted to tell his wife that for a moment, he thought it was Ameerah seated next to him, but he managed to swallow the words.

He drew her close and squeezed her shoulders.

"My Ameerah, she was smiling, and she had a gold tooth" Her voice was laden with sorrow. Alhaji Saleh felt pain in his heart.

"Do you think she is dead, Alhaji?"

He squeezed her shoulders again and waited for the pain in his chest to lessen. After a long sigh, he said in a whisper, "No. She will come home. She is close by, I can feel her presence. Let's get some sleep."

Rite of Passage

- Mojola Oluwa

As I felt our plane leave the runway of the Maiduguri International Airport, I looked out of the window and saw everything receding as we went higher. I laughed drily and the lady beside me looked at me suspiciously. I almost apologised for making her uncomfortable but I was not in the mood to entertain any questions or offer any explanations so I reached for my headsets and wore them, not because I wanted to listen to any music but just so I would not be involved in the discussion that I saw rearing its head. I wanted my solitude. I wanted to mourn the loss of my innocence. I wanted to bury myself and the gory details of the past couple of months.

I was done with adventures. I now understood why it was easier for most people to ignore the craze and pretend everything was alright instead of choosing to deal with rot.

I remembered when I left Ibadan about nine weeks earlier. My parents had resignedly let me go when I told them that I had volunteered to work in the Internally Displaced Persons (IDP) Camp in Borno.

My mother initially kicked against it vehemently, but I had played the moral card. I told her that I wanted to do what we had always been taught to do - do unto others what you want them to do to you. If the South had been attacked like those in the North had been, we would have wanted to know that people were out there looking out for us and helping in every way they could. Reluctantly they had agreed to let me go after making sure I had taken every shot of vaccine I possibly could get.

I was the Red Cross Commander in my school while I was an undergraduate and so it was easy for me to go through the platform of the Red Cross. I had completed my studies in law since the month of December of last year. By the time of our graduation, it was late for us to meet the first semester in Law School. So my classmates and I had to wait till October of the next year before proceeding to the Law School. I had wondered all year round about what to do with such an amount of free time on my hands. Then I recalled how Immanuel, my best friend and I always joked about going to Borno and living there as volunteer humanitarian workers. And so it began, my quest for adventure.

On the day I left home, my mother was almost in tears. I wondered why she was worried since I was going to be away for only six months. I was not leaving the country and the Red Cross provided maximum security for their volunteers and the IDP camps were heavily guarded, what could possibly go wrong?

Immanuel had followed our truck to the airport and we joked about a lot of things on the way. When we arrived at the Camp, I felt a jolt of reality hit me. I saw over a million faces of people in despair looking towards our truck as it drove past them to our tent. I saw naked children scampering as our truck moved in their direction. When we got down from the truck, I couldn't quite tell if it was the stench of human excreta that hit my nostrils first or the thick dust that welcomed me, but I felt a wave of nausea hit me. I wasn't quite certain about my resolve anymore, but it was too late to back out. I was shown to my corner. All I was given were a flat mattress on the bare floor under a mosquito net. There was also a bucket in the corner. That was all.

I changed into my uniform and headed to the clinic. As a volunteer we had been taught to be as empathic as we could but not to get attached to any of the victims. We were also taught to wash our hands after attending to any of them. We were reminded of our basic first aid procedures and routines. Work began immediately and I plunged myself into it.

My first friend was Chief. I noticed him on the first day. He was hard to miss. I had seen how unlike the others he did not go to queue to get his food and so I thought it was because his left leg was amputated. I later discovered that he actually did not stand up for anything and he got a special treatment for everything and so I decided to ask a lady in the camp who seemed to know why. She told me in whatever English she could speak that he used to be the chief in their community before the insurgents attacked their village. On the night the village was attacked, the lady told me, the chief had fought bravely to lead as many of them as he could through an escape route he had discovered. He was hit by an axe but in spite of his injuries, he led them out of the danger. He had lost every member of his family while trying to save the people. He was really respected by his people.

While in the camp, I focused on treating little bruises and dressing wounds and getting to know my patients. They all called me Doctor. Soon enough I found out that my queue always was longer than other queues. Mrs Ogazie, a senior colleague, told me it was a good sign that I was doing a good job and that the people were beginning to trust me. I felt a surge of pride and was motivated to do more.

One day, Rachael, another volunteer like me came to whisper in my ears that my attention was required. I followed her to the back of the tent where we met our excited colleagues. Rachael told me that the Red Cross was paying us some bonuses. I received my envelope happily. I got twenty-five thousand naira, it was not an awful lot but I was richer.

Before I slept that night, I wondered why we were given the bonuses. We were told there were no financial rewards at all and it was okay by me. I also wondered why we had to hide behind the tent to receive our bonus.

I woke up the next morning to shouts coming from outside the tent. I got up hurriedly and ran out to see the cause of the fracas. I saw a woman holding Mr. Bala, the Red Cross commander at this camp by the trouser and shaking him violently.

'You this thief! You think you can double-cross me here *abi*? I will show you pepper.'

'Shameless idiot! You know this is the second time *eh*? If you try it again, I will go to the media, call me a bastard if I don't. Stupid people.''

She pushed him back with so much force that he landed with a crash on his backside. She looked at the rest of us like she wanted to descend on us, then with a loud hiss she walked away.

'*EhnEhn*...what are you people looking at? Come on...will you get out of this place,' Mr. Bala managed to say after the woman had left and we all scampered back into our tents.

I couldn't believe my ears as Rachel narrated the full details of what transpired that morning.

'My dear, that's how it happens here-o. I don't know why the woman was shouting. It is first come, first served. After all, she has also done it to us too. Once when *Oga* was the one that brought the big fish, she used woman power to corner him and she did not even share with her group. Only her, chop and clean mouth.'

I tried to mask my shock but obviously I was failing because she looked at me and laughed.

'But aren't these funds supposed to go to the agency or the government or the appropriate authority for the welfare of these victims?'

'*Hian*. Government *ko*? Don't you know if it enters government pocket it won't come out? Or is it the government that works here? Is it the government that brings in the donors? *Biko*, leave authorities out of this matter! It is fastest fingers first. *Oga* is just a nice man; other leaders don't share with their followers. Do you know he is a man of God? That's why he is so honest. *Chai,* God bless that man."

I was bewildered. Was she really that ignorant of what they were doing or she had just managed to convince herself it wasn't such a bad thing.

Later that afternoon, I saw Mrs. Ogazie turn back some patients, telling them to come back the next day. I went to meet her and asked her what the problem was, she told me that we had run out of anti-malaria drugs and all we had left were Paracetamol and Vitamin C tablets, some bottles of Methylated Spirit and a lot of Cotton wool packs. So we had to censor the cases to entertain, 'minor illnesses like malaria should be given Paracetamol tablets and a cold bath.'

I asked how long this 'draught' period was going to last and she said till the end of the month. It was the eighth of June.

When Fatima brought her mother to the clinic that afternoon, I was dressing a wound. I noticed her immediately she walked in, holding her mother by the side but I had learnt to mind my business. But when I heard arguments ensue. I was surprised at the impeccable command of English language she expressed. I had to listen carefully.

'How can you tell me to take her back after all I explained to you?'

'Madam, you cannot leave her here. We have no drugs for her and we can't just admit her here. Take her back to your tent.'

'You would have to do that over my dead body. You think I don't know what you people are supposed to be doing? You think I don't know what to do? I would shout, I would start a protest in this camp if you don't find something to do about this. What am I supposed to do?'

She began to cry and her tears made everyone uncomfortable. One after another, they left the room after a while.

I finished with my patient and moved to sit beside her. She looked at me and I could see that we were roughly about the same age but she looked so much older around the eyes.

'You know, I don't care about anything that happens anymore. I have seen more deaths in the past six months than I ever thought possible. I have lost everything...my father, my siblings, my friends, my pride, my faith, everything. Just look at her, dying right before my eyes and there's nothing I can do. Do you know there's no food in the camp right now? Do you know that these officials hoard the remaining portions and give them out in exchange for sexual favours?' laughing drily when my eyes expanded in shock.

'You are too naïve for this place. You should go back home before you lose it like me,' she told me sternly.

'I…I just came to help out. We need to change how things are done around here. We can't give up on this system,' I said in defence although the words sounded weak even to my own ears.

'I am sorry if I don't share your enthusiasm.'

She got up from her seat to leave.

'Please can you watch her for me for a couple of minutes? I need to go get us some food,' she told me.

'I thought you said there was no food in the camp anymore?'

'There's food for those of us without shame.'

Then she left.

I later got close to Fatima over the next couple of weeks. I learnt that her father was an Army Commander and he had been killed in an ambush laid by the Boko Haram sect. That was the beginning of their travails as a family. The other members of the family had also been killed during an attack on their community. From her family, only Fatima and her mother escaped alive. They had to spend some time hiding in the forest on their journey to the camp, a snake had bitten Fatima's mother. A local snake charmer had applied some herbs to the spot but that was not enough. After a couple of weeks, she began to experience severe headaches and general fatigue. After a series of tests, it was discovered that the local antidote might not have been completely effective.

Fatima was a final year student in the University of Borno before the whole insurgency began.

The first thing I did was to volunteer to personally care for Fatima's mother. I can still remember the way Mr Bala looked at me and told me to be very careful and to mind my business. But I wasn't to be deterred, my mind was made up. I managed to pitch some money together, my personal money, raised some from my parents, started a go-fund-me account and I was able to get a lot of money.

Another thing I managed to do was to make enemies. I was told clearly to mind my business and stop getting personal with the victims. I was also accused of trying to make everybody else look bad. But every time I saw young ladies enter the rooms of the male officials, every time I saw bodies being packed, every time I saw little children with their ribs poking out of their flesh, I knew I could not stop thinking about ways that I could be of help to them.

Yesterday morning, after counting what I had gathered, I realised that I had enough to take Fatima's mother to the airport and transfer her to UCH in Ibadan for proper treatment. Under escort, I had gone to town to withdraw the money. I had returned with a big smile on my face. That was before I noticed the solemn appearance of everyone.

I recognised that aura, it was one that we dealt with every day and so I could not understand why I felt a slight shiver run down my spine. I stepped into the clinic and saw that everyone was looking at me with pitiful, wet eyes. Mrs. Ogazie looked at me and broke down in tears. My heart shattered because I knew what had happened. But when I heard Fatima's dry laughter ring out from the corner of the room, my legs shook.

I gave the money to Fatima and packed my bags that night. I knew it was time to go home.

The Pilot's landing announcement brought me out of my reverie. I got my bags and walked out. I saw Immanuel wave at me from afar and I felt a tear slip from my eyes because at that moment I knew something he didn't know. He had lost me.

I had lost myself.

Flying Over the Crises

- Audee T. Giwa[*]

"It is wrong of you, sir, to generalize and say all the non-governmental organizations were flying over the crises to go camp safely in one forest and go back to the international community to claim more funding. That others did this does not mean all of us are doing it."

The young lady made this rebuttal after Prof. Othman's postulations that most of the NGOs grew fat on the Nigeria's north-eastern crises of the Boko Haram without adequately doing anything commensurate with the funding they received to alleviate the suffering of the affected populace, especially the IDPs, the so-called Internally Displaced Persons.

Othman kept quiet for a while, knowing full well that as an academic, the woman had some point. You simply did not generalize especially on issues such as these. But what did this little girl know about suffering? What did she know about loss? Did she lose two sisters and a brother in one fell swoop? Was she ever made fugitive in her home? Was her house ever forcefully confiscated and turned into a den of terror by the insurgents? What could this pickaninny tell him or anyone about generalization? In fact was that even the issue?

"I am sorry, fellow panellists," Othman sobered up. "May I crave your indulgence to narrate Bulama's story here?"

---

[*] **Audee Giwa** is a Lecturer at the Department of English and Drama, Kaduna State University Kaduna. He has been visiting lecturer to Saudi Arabia and England.

Lola Shoneyin, the ebullient arbitrator, or chair of the panel if you will, first looked at members of the audience who were psyched into silence by Othman's sombre voice, and then turned to look at Othman himself. Was this north-eastern water beneath her depth? She heaved a long sigh and motioned for Othman to carry on.

"You may first wish to ask me, 'Who is Bulama?' The answer is simpler than the question. Bulama is an ordinary Nigerian from the north-east. He has just enough Western education to go by in these modern times. He was a teacher in one of the primary schools in Maiduguri. For a long while, the whole hue and cry about Boko Haram meant nothing to him. Whether it was a terrorist organization or a group of misguided miscreants deserved little of his attention. He was just going about his normal business of making ends meet, trying to feed his ageing parents and his two little daughters. If there was a bomb blast there, he would join in assisting the injured and burying the dead. For most dwellers of Maiduguri death had become a constant companion. No one any longer observed the respectful three days of mourning. For it was not inconceivable that as you were returning from the graveyard to bury the dead, another bomb blast would have occurred that would necessitate your going back to the funeral ground. Death had become almost commonplace. Dead bodies were a common sight. Bulama thought he was used to all these already.

"Then, one day he came home to find his own family gone. He was at his workplace when he heard the news that the insurgents had attacked that part of the town where his house was. A lot of people were feared dead. Thinking only for the safety of his daughters, he rushed home. He found the house deserted. His heart stood still. He did not know whether to shout or die. There was no one he could ask or talk to.

"He slumped at the entrance of his room muttering *inna lillahi wa inna ilaihir raji'un* - from God we came and unto Him is our returning.

"He did not know for how long he sat there. What he knew however was that someone came much later and was tapping him gently on his shoulders.

"*Sannu*, Bulama, *Sannu*."

It was Huzi, his neighbour.

'Take heart, my brother. Our parents are gone. They killed them all. I came too late."

Bulama shouted at Huzi.

'What do you mean? Whose parents are dead?' I just left *mama* and *baba* here. Don't tell me such nonsense.'

But even as he was screaming, Bulama knew that it was the truth. There had been so many deaths in recent times. And it did not really matter who died. Except that the pain of yours dying was always more unbearable than the pain of your neighbour's.

"In a calm and forcefully controlled voice he asked, 'And my wife and two children?'

'Safe in my house. But the insurgents killed my parents too.'

"It was doubtful if Bulama had heard Huzi's last statement. Like bullet shot from a gun, he bolted into Huzi's house and there found his two daughters and wife crying silently with the remaining members of Huzi's household."

"The sight was heart-wrenching. Bulama knew he could not stay another day in that town. Zombie-like, he motioned his family to follow him. Again, zombie-like, they obeyed. The numbness that so much inhumanity, so much cruelty and so much death, could wrought on the psyche of one family could best be imagined than stated.

"As they followed him out, he held Falmata's hand. She was his youngest, and therefore the dearest thing to his heart. They plunged into the house and packed very little of their belongings and proceeded out of the house and started walking the narrow path that linked their area with the main road.

"As Huzi stood there watching his friend and neighbour leave with his family, he felt the tears slowly run down his cheeks. He wished he could utter some words of consolation to Bulama. But his loss was not any less severe than his. So he let him be. Whatever happened, he was sure they would link up some other day.

"As provident would have it, a police vehicle on belated patrol picked up Bulama and his family. When asked where they were going, Bulama simply told the policemen 'West.'

"It was his wife Aisa, who was able to tell the police on patrol what they just went through. Bulama had told her while they were packing, that he was taking them to Zaria. How they would get there, no one knew.

"When the Inspector asked Bulama if he had any money, Bulama shook his head. The scene was emotionally charged. The policemen themselves had very little on them. But seeing the pathetic situation of the Bulama family, they each, without prompting, emptied what little they had and gave them to Bulama. Because it was getting late in the afternoon, the Inspector suggested that they should stay the night at the station. Bulama was beyond caring. What he knew for sure was that he was not going to sleep again in his family house ever again.

"He soon discovered that not only was he going to sleep ever in his family house again, it was very probable that he would never sleep in Borno State again. For, as they approached the police station, they saw the convoy of the Commissioner of police leaving for Kano. The Commissioner was kind enough to ask what was happening and upon being told, directed Bulama and his family to join one of his escort cars.

"Six hours later, they arrived Kano and Bulama heaved a sigh of relief. He knew that he had left the horrors of insurgency behind him.

"The strangest thing he found out was that the Commissioner had a guest house in Kano. Soon, he understood, it was not just the commissioner but other top government functionaries too. That constituted little of his problem at that point. The officials of his state were not less human than he was. Even where you had taken oath to protect the lives and property of other people, the protection of your own life came first. Surely, you had to be alive first to be able to render a helping hand to those in need. So temporarily the administrative headquarters of Borno became Kano.

"Anyhow, Bulama and his family slept in Kano in the luxurious guest house of the Police Commissioner. In the morning, a driver was detailed to take them to Zaria where Bulama hoped to trace a long lost acquaintance of his.

"In Zaria, the police escort who was unable to trace Bulama's friend, handed them over to the Samaru Divisional Police Officer (DPO). This man too was kindness personified. He asked Bulama if he had any money with which they could rent an apartment. Bulama told him that the Police Commissioner who brought them from Maiduguri had given him fifty thousand naira. Before then, the patrolling policemen who picked them up in Borno had contributed about eight thousand for them.

"The DPO told Bulama that he should hold on to his money. He would need it to feed his family before he got something to do. He also promised to assist him to get a house in the low brow area of Samaru otherwise called Hayin Dogo by the locals.

"Luck was again on their side, as the house the DPO took them belonged to his friend. Sergeant Alu, fondly called Sergeant by all, was a retired police officer, leaving humbly on his meagre pension and augmenting his income by selling secondhand clothes in Samaru market. Sergeant was poor by all standards. He was poor not because his income was too small, but because his family was too large. He had two wives and thirteen children. But his house was big and spacious.

"So when the DPO narrated Bulama's ordeals to him, Sergeant said they could stay for free till Bulama found something to do.

"This arrangement was convenient for all. And soon Bulama was employed as a Security Officer at one of the Health Clinics in Hayin Dogo. Still, Sergeant said Bulama should not pay any rent till he was fully settled. He gave him another six months of grace.

"It was at the expiry of the six months, when Bulama wanted to start making the payment to his benefactor that his wife called his attention to the fact that Falmata, their last child, now almost five years, was experiencing serious pain in her private parts whenever she wanted to urinate.

"Bulama rushed his daughter to the clinic where he was working and upon investigation it was discovered that she had been forcefully defiled. The wound and infection in her vaginal area were worsening by the day.

"Bulama was beside himself with sorrow when he learnt that his little girl had been repeatedly raped by the twenty-five-year old son of his benefactor, Saleh! The horror was beyond imagining. Saleh, the soft-spoken, kind Saleh who seemed to love Bulama's children as if they were his own blood sisters was a paedophile after all!

"Bulama had an unquestionable faith in the authorities. He dashed to the Samaru Divisional Police Headquarters and reported the incident while his daughter was receiving treatment at the clinic.

"The DPO was choking with anger. He instantly ordered the arrest of Saleh even before his friend, the Sergeant, came back from the market where he was selling his secondhand clothing. As soon as Saleh was brought before the DPO, the later was seen visibly restraining himself from committing instant murder.

"'Did you or did you not rape that poor girl whose family your own father has magnanimously given shelter to when they were in need?'

"Saleh hesitated.

"Just then the Sergeant dashed into the interrogation room and descended on his son beating, scratching, biting, and trying to strangle him all at once.

"The officers there tried to restrain him. He was foaming at the mouth, screaming unprintable obscenities and curses on his son. Everyone, Bulama among them, stood there watching. When his strength failed him the Sergeant slumped and began to sob.

"Bulama with the DPO stood over the Sergeant watching the unrepentant eyes of Saleh.'

"'Did you or did you not rape that poor girl?'"

"'I did,' Saleh said simply.

"'*Inna lillahi wa inna ilaihir raji'un*, ' Sergeant exclaimed. 'Saleh! May what you did to this poor girl be done to you. DPO, Sir. You have my permission. Let the law take its course!

"Bulama was still quiet as the DPO ordered Saleh to be transferred to the dreaded Kaduna Criminal Investigation Department of the Nigeria Police Force.

"As they took Saleh away, Bulama helped Sergeant up and together they walked silently to the clinic where Falmata was already showing good signs of recovery.

Professor Othman paused and looked at Lola Shoneyin, other panellists and finally at the audience and said, "Ladies and gentlemen, that was yesterday. Falmata is still in the hospital."

They Call Me Helen

- Hassana U. Maina*

It was in the dusk of harmattan when the *dogonyaro* tree swayed to the left and to the right producing an almost frigid temperature. The earth rose with vengeance, turning the hair and faces of pedestrians sand-like. The woman selling *akara* was attending to anxious children who were trying too much to get to school before Assembly time. The men who owned shops around traded, mostly sweets and biscuits, as if in a race with the breeze.

Everyone seemed aware that they were walking on a time bomb that might explode sooner than later. Death is a certainty to every human but what makes it bearable is the illusion of safety that humans over the years create for themselves. But the people of Biu local government did not seem to share this illusion with the rest of the world; they have realised that the guns and ammunitions soldiers and police carry around to protect them might as well be used to create terror.

Hyelni didn't grow up around toy guns. In fact at the time, toy guns were rare while the real ones were everywhere. She had witnessed more than once when a gun had been used to end people's lives, people to whom she had said *good morning*, *good afternoon* or other pleasantries expected of a well-trained 10-year-old girl. Many a time, when she dodged a bullet, she would say as her mother had taught her, *"Alhamdullilah"*, all

* **Hassana Umoru Maina** is from Borno State, Nigeria. She is a law student at the Ahmadu Bello University, Zaria. She is the current Chairperson of the Creative Writers Club, ABU, Zaria. She is presently working on her first novel.

praises to *Allah*. She was grateful for getting another second, minute or week to live.

On one occasion, Hyelni's social studies teacher digressed while teaching the pupils the values of life. He started talking to them about hope for the future and faith in God. Hyelni knew her teacher was saying nonsense. Hope was too enormous a concept for her brain to wrap round and she knew for a fact that none of those sitting in the class that moment believed Mrs. Aisha. Dahiru, the noisy boy that had a permanent seat in the front, died as a result of a bomb blast in the market. He was helping his mother sell *ugwu*. Amina, the girl that never seemed to understand anything in class, had been missing since last month and is yet to be found. Hyelni's bosom friend, Kucheli, had not been in school for almost two months because she was yet to overcome the trauma of being assaulted by insurgents that raided their house, ripped off her clothes and took turns with her. Aliyu died after a bomb was detonated in the mosque beside their house. From what Hyelni heard, Aliyu didn't want to go to the mosque that early but his mother insisted he had to start praying with the other men in the house.

Hyelni had not watched her classmates die but she witnessed the death of her brother and her father, and the abduction of her mother. Hyelni was squatting over the pit they used as toilet, answering the call of nature when the men entered her compound. Her father knew the insurgents were in their village as soon as sporadic gunshots were heard. But her parents, like the other people in the village, knew it was futile to run, and so whenever the insurgents came, they muttered to death "not today", like Arya does in the movie, *Game of Thrones*. But it seemed like death came with a mind of its own when the insurgents slaughtered Hyelni's brother and father like rams. Only that they cut them through the back of their necks, and forced Hyelni's mother into the back of their truck. Hyelni saw all of that through the holes on the toilet's zinc door.

The last she remembered were her eyes hovering round her father's lifeless body and her brother's head detached from his entire frame. She woke up to lots of people around her. As she made to sit up, Maman Kucheli, the oldest woman in the village gave her a pitiable look and gestured her to lay still. Hyelni knew what all that was about. She could feel the remnant of the unfinished business she was doing in the toilet still stuck in her anus. She made to sit up again, and this time, many eager hands helped her up. She walked outside and heard some of the women talking in hushed tones. They talked about how lucky Hyelni was to have survived and how God had plans for her.

Hyelni was just seven but it seemed to her that she might be the only logical person in the whole village. She wasn't lucky. She could see that there was really nothing worth living for. Just when she reached for the door of the toilet, everything dawned on her. She knew her brother and father were dead; she was sure they had been buried when she passed out. She was unsure of what they did to her mother.

She wanted to cry, but the tears just would not form. Her eyes were clear, white and still. The questions that kept going through her mind did not have to do with her parents or her brother. It had to do with her. She taunted her young mind with the questions about who she was, what her life was worth, and where she was going or who she was moving in with.

For the first time, she understood what the word, orphan, meant. To be an orphan is to be alone in a crowded market, to have no one to share a name or a unique feature with. She knew she would never see her brother again but wished God could bring him back, even if for only three days. *He had done it before*, she thought. *Is that not what he did with Jesus?* She questioned herself. She heard Mrs. Christie say so when she was teaching Christian religion knowledge to some pupils. She thought Mrs Christie was just bluffing, but right now she really wanted to believe it was possible. She would give anything to have her brother back; she promised God that if he ever brought her brother back, she would never get angry with anyone that comments on how much they looked alike or cry when her father praises her brother's school work over hers.

"I should have clapped louder when Ali got 100% in mathematics," she said aloud.

She remembered her father, how he woke up every morning to clean his motorcycle that was already rusting away, and how her mother used to tell him that with the kind of smoke that the motorcycle produced, he should not bother telling people that he does not smoke cigarette.

As her legs started to ache, she realised she had been squatting over the pit for far too long. She hurriedly washed up and walked outside. She saw the mortar and pestle her mother had washed just some hours back and remembered how everyone was excited about the thought of eating pounded yam for dinner. She closed her eyes and imagined how her mother would be pounding the yam and sweat oozing out from her forehead, yet would still manage to throw her head back and laugh in a way only she could. Before she opened her eyes, she made a mental note never to eat pounded yam again, she would not want to ever feel this way.

A week later, Hyelni along with few other orphans were taken to a charity foundation in Lagos. The prospect of travelling to another part of the country brought smile and laughter to the faces of the children, but not Hyelni. The reality of starting a new life felt good; she'd completely let go of the past. She knew she was never coming back to the place she had always known as home yet she didn't want to carry anything along with her. A day before they travelled, she burnt her favourite dress, the one her father bought for her after she cried and begged him. She threw her mother's wristwatch in the river. The only thing she carried along with her was her brother's favourite pencil, and that is because she hid it from him days before he was killed, and when she felt it in her jeans, she held on to it for a while. As they passed the route leaving Maiduguri to Yobe, she threw it out through the window.

When they got to Lagos, the only thing she couldn't get over was the familiar faces of the other children. So, she deliberately tried to mismatch their names and faces. Whenever anyone tried to correct her, she replied with "Okay, big head." Soon, she had made herself an enemy to all the kids she travelled with and she also succeeded in making half of the kids she met in Lagos hate her. The first Yoruba words she learnt were hate words, and she reserved every new insult she learnt for the other kids at the Foundation. And to the other kids that did not understand Hausa, she relished in saying despicable things to them in Hausa.

She refused to utter a word about what happened to her parents and that bothered Mrs. Adebisi, the director of Charity Foundation who made it a routine to call Hyelni to talk to her. But whenever she asked her about her parents, all Hyelni said was "They are dead."

When the proprietor of Queens' Only Boarding School wrote to offer full scholarship to one of the orphans, she knew which one to let go. But to be fair, she decided to give the girls at her foundation a mathematics test. Hyelni knew all the answers, but she left her paper blank. A week after the test, Mrs. Adebisi announced that Hyelni passed and she will be going to Queens' Only Boarding School. At that moment, Hyelni knew Mrs. Adebisi wanted to get rid of her. For the first time, since her loss, she let a tear fall. Mrs. Adebisi saw her fighting tears and invited her to her office.

"You will come back for holidays," Mrs. Adebisi told her while stroking her back. "I felt a new environment with girls from different backgrounds would be good for you."

Hyelni didn't say anything; she just thanked her and left. She wasn't one to relish in a bad situation for long.

On her first day at Queens' Only, she realised she had to change almost everything about herself to fit in. She heard names she had never heard before. There was an Amarachi, Chinenye, Busayo, Ife and so many strange names she didn't even bother pronouncing. And all the girls she met seemed anxious to change her name from Hyelni to Helen; she tried to argue at first but when she realised that pronouncing Hyelni was as much a torture to them as pronouncing their names was to her, she decided to give in.

The Monday after she resumed, she went to the administration office to complete her registration. The lady at the front desk asked for her name and she said 'Helen Abdullahi.' That was her first mistake. When the lady reached the box for religion, she ticked Christianity without consulting her, and that was when it really struck Hyelni. What religion does she really belong to? Her parents were Muslims, but she had not been a Muslim since she came to Lagos, in fact she had not been a Christian either. She realised just how futile it would have been to protest, so she kept quiet and decided that being a Christian wouldn't be a bad idea after all.

English class was the first she attended at the school. Miss Badiru, their teacher, asked them to write an essay about their family. The next day Miss Badiru came to the class smiling, called Helen out and told the class how impressed she was with Helen's essay and asked Helen to read out her essay before the class. Everything Helen wrote in that essay was fabricated. She wrote that she was an only child of a Major-General in the Nigerian Army and her mother was a medical doctor. She wrote stories about the defeat of the insurgents at the hands of her fabricated father which he had supposedly told her. When she finished reading the story, a loud applause shook the class. She became everyone's friend; even those she didn't like tried everything to be on her list of favoured persons.

At the end of that term, Helen knew she had to find a way to avoid the foundation's bus from coming to pick her, because if that ever happened, everyone would know she was a scam. She knew the bus would come to her school only through one route, so when they were dismissed, she carried the small duffle bag in which she kept her few possessions and snuck out of the school through the school fence. She passed Royal Hospital, passed the sloppy road and got to Sabo market. There she waited to ambush the bus. At exactly 3:05 pm, the bus got to her and she waived it to a stop.

Hyelni returned to the foundation with the mindset that everyone there hated her. But the moment she entered, she realised how wrong she had been. Most of the kids were no longer there; they got families to adopt them. Instead, they were new faces. And with what Hyelni could decipher from their faces, they were excited to meet her. She stopped picking fights and would gather the other children that didn't come from Maiduguri and tell them lies about how she had killed a man with a stick and covered him with leaves. Her real intent of telling them the stories was to make them fear her, but she fascinates them instead. So they spent all their time around her like little puppies around a bitch. Soon her holiday rolled out, and another term came.

At fifteen and in JSS3, Helen's had grown into a tall beauty.

Mr Oseni, her English teacher, took a special interest in her after he read a poem she had written behind her English notebook:

I suspected myself of insanity
For amidst my tears
I searched for you
Hundred years gone
You were as close to my heart
As a child to his mother's breast
Oh! Forgotten love
Memories of you are now in oblivion

The sound of your name is
As unclear as the rage of
the ocean in a strong wind

He invited her to read the poem to him. That was the beginning of their friendship. He would call her to the staffroom under the pretence of extra tutorials, and they would talk until she had exhausted her free periods. He never told her a thing about himself, but he listened to all she had to say about herself. She told him nothing but the truth.

After a while, curious Hyelni asked Mr Oseni to tell her about himself. He laughed and said, "I can't tell you about myself without crying my eyes out. And I wouldn't want to cry in the staffroom."

He asked her to meet him outside school at night and she didn't hesitate to answer in the affirmative.

At 8pm, she sneaked out of school through the fence as they had earlier planned; he was waiting to receive her. She changed into the clothes she had brought along. They passed all the restaurants around Yaba, but he didn't stop. She got a little worried but shrugged it off with the thought that he might want to take her to a place with fewer eyes. He drove to a motel on Bode Thomas in Surulere. When he stopped at the motel, Hyelni tried not to flinch but fear was written on her face. She was just fifteen, but she knew she had reasons to be scared.

"Don't be scared," he said, correctly reading her thoughts. "No one can ever find us here." He paid for a room and got a key. When he opened the room, Hyelni sat on a creaking chair and tried to take an inventory of the room. The room smelt of cheap air freshener; the white bed sheet had obvious stains. He sat down on the bed and faced her.

"My Father died before I was born," he started, nudging her to rest on his chest. "And my mother only lived long enough to hear me cry or so I was told. My aunt took me in and as soon as I could walk, she started to maltreat me. She would beat me over every little thing I did wrong and would give me spoilt food whenever I complained of hunger."

He continued. Helen looked at him, he was crying. As she moved closer to him, he drew her to sit on his laps.

"*Shhh*," she tried to comfort him.

He grabbed her and buttoned her dress from the top. She tried to stop him but another part of her wanted to see how far that would go. When she had no clothes on again and he had removed his pair of trousers, she realised what she was up against.

"No!" she screamed but there was no going back. His hands already covered her mouth and his hands were busy undressing her. She had never felt so much physical pain before. His weight on her was suffocating her, but he didn't care. Her body was ripped into two – or so she felt.

Mr. Oseni never spoke to Helen about what happened between them. It even seemed as though he was avoiding her. On one of the Mondays that followed, Helen was in the staffroom when she heard the teachers talking about why Mr. Oseni had been unavailable. They all agreed that it was because his wife had returned from her trip overseas. Helen left the staffroom, without getting the book she had gone there for. She could not believe that Mr. Oseni had a wife. She regretted her relationship with him and wished the ground could open up and swallow her. She thought of meeting him for explanation. After she analysed everything, she thought otherwise and concluded that she did not deserve any explanations. After all, she is yet to understand why she has lost her entire family. She buried whatever had happened between her and Mr. Oseni, and promised herself never to relive it.

The problem with burying things is that you would not know how it would spring up on you. After two months of not seeing her menstrual flow, she knew she was pregnant. She did not know what to think of at that point. All she could think about was how the insurgents had changed her destiny.

Dashed Hopes
(for the Nyanya blast)

- Safiya Ismaila Yero

Reluctantly, she dragged herself out of bed and headed for the bathroom. She had to get up early enough so as to use the bath early to avoid the long bathroom queue. She lived in a rented room and parlour with her five children and had to share a kitchen and a bathroom with seven other families. She was lucky to be the second on the queue that day. Ola, a graduate desperately searching for a job, had beaten her to it. He was the son of a fellow tenant, a retired guard who they call Baaba. Baaba had taken ill two months earlier. There was no money to even feed his family of eight all living in a room and parlour talk more of taking Baaba to the hospital. So Baaba remained at home and took malaria drugs and Panadol, sometimes with IbuProfen if he complained of his aching bones. Ola often rubbed *Aboniki* balm on his father's limbs. He knew he had to get a job, and fast too. After all Baaba invested so much in him by sending him to university. He was now the messiah of the family. But every day for two years on, he had bathed, taken his brown envelope at the break of dawn and returned at dusk with the same story: no job. He wished he could repeat his National Youth Service. At least then he was getting some change.

"Mama Aysha, hope you slept well," he greeted, as he stepped out of the door-less bathroom.

"Yes, we thank God, Ola. How is Baaba's health?" she asked as she picked her pail of water.

"He is better. I'll be taking him to the hospital this morning. We have to leave early enough to beat the Nyanya traffic," he replied with a wan smile, a ray of hope flashing through his dark sad eyes.

Mama Aysha, as Halima was popularly called, understood. He must have got some money to take Baaba to the hospital. Thank God. She did not know that Baaba was the one taking Ola somewhere, and not the other way round as she was told, and not to the hospital as well. Baaba wanted to take Ola to his former Boss to beg him to purchase a tricycle or motor cycle for him to pay in instalments.

When she came out of the bathroom, she met Mama Okpa waiting her turn.

"Mama, hope you slept well. Please let me have two hundred naira *okpa* before you leave," she requested and went to her room.

The aroma of *okpa* filled the air. Mama Okpa's wheelbarrow was already washed and left to drain against the wall, ready for today's business. When the *okpa* was ready, Mama *okpa* would pour the hot *okpa* into a big white polythene bag and place it in the wheel barrow, which she would push and shout "*okpa!*" at intervals until she got to the Nyanya park, where most of it usually got sold.

"Aysha, when your brothers and sister are up, draw water from the well, wash yourselves, pray and eat the *okpa* in the food flask. There is also *akamu* in the yellow rubber. I won't be long."

"Mama, are you bringing the sewing machine today?"

Mama Aysha didn't know how to answer her daughter. She had told her about the sewing machine last week. She had equally promised her she would teach her to sew, just as she was taught by her mother. But she had never had any reason to sew in the twelve years that she has been married. Baba Aysha had said there was no need; after all he had always sent money for their upkeep because he was hardly around. The very last time he came, he had promised they would move to their new apartment, which he was building at Kurudu, which was why he could not afford to waste money renting a bigger place.

She could clearly remember that he bought the land in Kurudu and started building the house when he came back from Peace Keeping in Liberia. Later he was posted to the mystical Boko Haram front in Borno, where he lost his life. She had spoken to him a few hours before he died, and he had told her he would send some money through a colleague the next day, that he would be home for a few days the following week.

They said it was an ambush. He was gone forever. No more coming home for naming ceremonies or *Eid* celebrations. No more homecoming to get her pregnant. No more money for upkeep. Yet, she still had to feed five mouths, and pay school fees. She didn't go beyond Primary school herself so; a job was out of the question. So she finally opted for sewing, an area which she was thought she could handle well. But she had no money for a sewing machine then. So she had asked a friend who had two and wanted to sell one on instalment payment. The friend had consented and promised to send the machine through her husband's brother who owned a tricycle popularly known as Keke Napep. That was three weeks ago, and still, nothing. Mama Aysha decided to check her up and use the little money she had left to transport the machine back home.

She took a motorcycle to the motor park. She was surprised to meet Mama Okpa already at the park with half of the *okpa* gone. Ola waved at her from the window of one of the long commercial buses popularly referred to as 'El Rufai' buses. She saw a *kabu-kabu* calling out for A.Y.A; which she boarded. She would alight at Kugb...suddenly the world came to an end. There was an earthquake and the sky was falling. The doors of hell were opened, vomiting fire...and she died...

*****

She slowly closed her eyes again. No! She wanted to die. Why would they tell her she was alive? Why should she live? She died once when she was told, coldly, over the phone, of her husband's death. She died again when the earthquake they now called bomb blast happened. Her daughter, Aysha, was holding her left hand, her face, tear stricken.

"Mama, thank God!"

Mama Aysha looked at her daughter. She realized that she looked much older than the last time she saw her. Her eleven year old daughter now looked eighteen.

"Where are your brothers and sister?" Mama Aysha finally managed to ask.

"With Aunty Maimuna. She brought me here the day it happened. She has brought the sewing machine for you. It's at home. You shall get well soon and teach me to sew, right, Mama?"

Mama Aysha felt a thousand needles of the sewing machine piercing through her heart, her brain, and all over her body. How could she even answer Aysha? She looked at the sheet covering her to the waist. How could she ever sew, when the blast had taken away her legs? How?

"Mama, thank God you are alive. Ola, Mama Okpa and Baaba are all dead, burnt in the blast."

Mama Aysha looked away and said nothing. She didn't know whether to thank God for keeping her alive without limbs or to beg Him to take her to the great beyond...

The Long and Empty Road

- Mnguember Vicky Sylvester

'There is always something to distinguish a Taiye from a Kehinde,' said Olu as the newscaster ended with a commentary on those who had left the PDP for the APC to welcome the president to Ogun state.

'And that is?' Chinedu asked sardonically, lacing his shoes.

It had been a long drive from the forest of death and he was hungry. Funny he didn't realise how hungry he was. He didn't even notice the breeze that now caressed his face. That is what fear does he mused, looking at and trying to ignore a healthy beggar.

'PDP and APC. Look at the former governors in PDP now Ministers in APC. Two faces of the same coin. Only exclusion was the president. He does not know their tricks of destruction which have continued after the sixteen years he complains about. Listen to clouds. They are silent on this menace the country faces. They feel safe in their high walled, guarded houses in Abuja and the rest depend on prayers. But this is good for the prayer warriors who need no work to earn big money. It is no wonder my driver left to train as a pastor. He told me he was 'tired of hustling.' The pastorate road is now more travelled...Olu chuckled .

'You must confess prayers brought us out of Sambisa,' Chinedu said with a frown.

'Baga I think,' Olu said, remembering his last flight in a fruitless attempt to reclaim the town from the insurgents.

'Whichever. What is the difference? We were picked at a checkpoint. Just like that and no one could resist.'

Chinedu was beginning to show signs of anger.

'Anyhow, everyone should be given arms with permits for protection. Does one need a licence to protect oneself? Someone is likely to give you reasons why we can't be permitted to have a gun though we saw those herders with guns. There are always excuses for allowing one and denying the other. It reminds one of the child that was asked to make a sentence with sugar and proudly answered, 'I drank tea this morning.' Olu smiled, 'Those you saw on the roads with arms have to protect their animals from rustlers and unfriendly terrains.'

As they connected the major pot-holed road with cars driving past, both men mourned with relief.

'Here we are,' Olu sighed looking at the long stretch of road before them as he recalled their narrow escape from the Camp. He scratched his head realizing he had not taken a bath in two days. He could not even recount his experience well enough to tell another. However, he knew that his wife had a way of dragging every bit of information out of him with her endless questions. He was sure that when he meets her she would make him recount his story. She would go like, where there non-Nigerians there? Where there many young women there? Did any helicopters drop anything while you were there? What were the ages of those trained to bomb themselves? How were they convinced? She was never short of questions that helped him recall things he could have ignored. A wise man says the ears that refuse to listen to advice go with the head when it is chopped off. He dropped his phone on Chinedu's legs and asked him to call family members.

Chinedu had joined him for lunch at his home from where they would leave for their trip. He had a week of his leave to spend with friends who were expecting him in Bauchi. Chinedu had decided to go with him as they had both lived in Bauchi and also thought it would be refreshing getting back there after several years. He said he would drive when Olu told him he had laid off his driver. The two of them had had their last meal in Olu's house about half an hour before they left Kano for Bauchi. Olu's wife had insisted they eat more than necessary and not to offend her, they had reluctantly eaten the side dishes and fruits. It was his luck, Chioma thought.

They had left Hotoro sure they would be in Bauchi before four o'clock. The road was not busy and they had not spent much time at the checkpoints where Olu would reveal his identity with some camaraderie slangs and they would be quickly waved on. A few times they had spotted the policemen pocket money that exchanged hands between them and motorists. The car belonged to Olu but Chinedu had insisted on driving knowing that for some time now Olu was driven long distances by the driver who had now left to become a pastor. Nothing wrong with that! After all, Christ's disciples were carpenters, fishermen and...they effectively caught men for Christ and became Saints and powerful reference points.

The problem with Olu's driver was that of one whose tongue was too free from the ropes of caution. Chinedu wished the preachers could reach out to Baga and the forest. Here are people who could not make one hair on their own heads wasting God's creation. But then one had to realise that God's creations were made of good and evil and Chinedu wondered if the evil could be totally weeded out of those whose DNA was evil-loaded...His wife had always argued that that God accepted people and judged them by their beliefs...Who knows? He sighed.

He remembered how heartily one of their kidnappers, Mustapha, had laughed following radio news that seven hundred soldiers were killed as they drove to the forest. He had thumbed his chest and looked at Adamu his partner who had kept his eye on the empty road, his mouth tightly shut. It was like a warning to a child not to grow his teeth longer than his lips. The military seem unable to cope with the insurgents, some people claimed, because the insurgents were better equipped being supported by France, ISIS and, even the government, through the money paid for kidnapped school girls.

Adamu was satisfied that government was not doing much to dispel these claims giving credence to Achebe's saying that he who gathers ant infested firewood, invites lizards to his house. If government gives amnesty, pay and absorb hoodlums into the army, does it not 'hate its brother and thus is in darkness and walking in darkness?' Things were not as easy as people believed, Adamu had thought. At the same moment, Chinedu was wondering why these men had killed some people who made attempts to escape. One of those people killed in an effort to escape was a core northerner. Was he not their brother? But who is the brother here...?

Chinedu's thoughts were in sync with Adamu's thoughts as he wondered why a clean, well-educated man of Adamu's age would go killing innocent people picked on the highways. He did not want to pursue that line of brotherhood as it seemed to make no meaning here.

He shifted his thoughts to Olu's endless jokes just before they met the hoodlums. They were laughing hard at an obscene proverb of rapists eating bearded meat of abducted women when they had suddenly stopped behind a car at a sharp corner. It was a miracle to have applied the breaks on time to avoid ramming into the car ahead of them. They noticed a line of vehicles ahead. They had thought it was another checkpoint but it was not long before two men and a boy of about ten came out of the car in front of them and were virtually pushed to the ground by two armed men in military uniform. The two from the car lay face down on the grass next to their car. It was obviously a scene of armed robbers.

'Look at their shoes...We are in trouble,' Olu said as the uniformed men walked towards them. They could see another armed boy frisk the men on the grass asking questions but Olu and Chinedu could barely hear them.

'Were from?' one asked as they got to Chinedu still behind the wheel.

'Kano,' Chinedu replied. They looked into the car as more uniformed men moved past them to the cars behind them.

'What is your job...you, no...you,' they asked in Hausa.

The two men kept silent.

One of the men whom they were to later know as Adamu said, 'looks like they don't understand.'

At that point the one later identified as Mustapha shouted, 'step back, there's a snake?'

The two men looked at him without moving.

'I think they don't understand,' one said. Just then a teenager with a Green Eagles T shirt ran up to them with a signal to hurry up. The man who had asked 'what job' opened the car and pulled Chinedu out as the other ran to the passenger door and got Olu out. They were pushed down and frisked hurriedly. Money and phones were taken and dropped into a back sack which contained purses, wristwatches, phones, jewellery. Olu was glad they had not asked him to remove his shoes. He had a few things there that could come handy in a getaway effort.

The operation took about half an hour. It was not long before Olu noticed the gun belonging to Mustapha was a toy. The one with Adamu, an AK47 was real and looked new. Adamu was young, about 33, slim but strong. He had an air of a comfortable background unlike his teammate who was younger, dirty but obviously strong. He looked hungry and short-tempered, kicking at Chinedu's foot that was in his way as he made his way to the back of the car and tried in vain to open the boot of the car.

'Get up and open the boot,' Adamu said to no one in particular.

Olu got up and walked towards Mustapha trying not to look where he had carefully placed his loaded rifle. It was just under the car by the driver's side. Tied to it was a phone fully charged but switched off. Adamu had frisked and collected their phones and money, threw out the foot mats as he checked under the seats and sun shield. He had emptied the computer bag on the back seat checking its contents which included a hundred thousand naira.

'What's this' he pointed to the inverter and battery.

Olu explained.

'We will go with them. We need this,' he said to his partner in Hausa. An older man of between 40 and 45 years walked briskly to the car and talked to Adamu, who turned and signalled to Olu and Chinedu to get into the car. The older man hurried to the next car.

It was not long before they could see that they were in a convoy of six cars. From Mustapha and Adamu's conversation they had left a few boys behind to pretend to be victims and to monitor events when the police arrived. A man called Jubrila in the police had called to inform the middle-aged man that some people had called the Commissioner and other high-ranking people and there was pressure on the police in Kano and Bauchi to send armed patrol. With this early information they had quickly rounded up the operation and abducted selected people and their cars. Olu was to later hear on arrival at the camp that several people were killed for resisting the kidnappers or those found to be soldiers and policemen.

The convoy drove half the night on a fairly good road through abandoned villages and then the forest. The cars stopped a few times for people to come down one car after the other to 'piss.' Olu tried to identify his location but it appeared like searching for a black goat in the darkness.

The lonely road seemed to have developed a character of its own. It seemed to moan or mourn whenever they stopped. The shrubs swished and whistled messages only they could understand and this seemed to build multiple sadness in the kidnapped. It was obvious the herbs were also indifferent to any herbalist out early to pick them. Herbs hated death around them and when it happened close by, herbalists stayed home because they knew the herbs would not respond to their calls. They especially detested those that urinated on them and often marked them out for revenge. Olu watched the bushes Adamu urinated on and felt sorry that the greens would soon receive their own. Olu's grandmother had repeatedly warned them and showed them as kids how to recognize powerful weeds and avoid annoying them. They healed but they were also vengeful.

Olu was still thinking of the herb Adamu had urinated on when the convoy turned off the lonely road into a bush path that seemed well-used by cars. On this narrow road the bushes aggressively caressed the windscreen as the cars drove on. No one took the trouble to trim the hedges that grew tall and folded towards the path. They were on this path for about twenty minutes when the cars suddenly slowed down and stopped. Adamu commanded the two men to come down and follow Mustapha while he took the rear pointing his rifle menacingly. They walked further into the bushes and suddenly they could see dim lights in a few places. They had arrived the camp.

Olu could see women preparing meals and he guessed for the new arrivals. He had heard Adamu talk to some about hunger and Mustapha had asked if no one had found even biscuits in a car. The women could be seen doing one thing or the other but it was rather dark for Olu to map out the surrounding. The room into which they were pushed contained other people, including a man and his wife and a pretty girl who kept her face down not even bothering about the new arrivals. A few people nodded to others in greeting and some managed twisted grins as a show of appreciation for the greeting.

Olu sat next to a man with his back against the wall and his legs stretched before him, his palms pressed on his knees. It seemed an effort for him to lift his hand for the handshake but seemed a bit relaxed after he had managed it.

'We were just taken today. How long have you been here,' Olu asked him.

'Three days sitting, sleeping. Waiting for the ransom to be paid.'

'Food? Olu asked.

'Once a day. I think they put something in the food to make us sleep most of the day. At night we are awake but shortly after a meal in the morning everyone sleeps. And when we wake up in the evening some of us are not here. It is assumed their ransom is paid and they have gone home. I am not sure,' he concluded sadly.

As they talked two men walked in and picked the beautiful girl. She walked with difficulty. Her name the new arrivals gathered was Maureen and several times a day she was taken out. Her crime was being so pretty. They all wanted her. Her parents had paid a ransom but they would not let her go; she was a slave, they said. *When did we turn from humans to this*, Chinedu thought as he listened to Maureen's story. He hung his head in shame. Olu nudged him.

'Engage them in conversation. You don't hide your nakedness from the person who will give you the last bath after death or show you the escape route.'

They did not touch the food that was brought to them. They had to be awake to the happenings or at least the whispers. The man who sat with his wife muttered as he looked at Olu, 'it is the heat of the fire that gave crayfish a bent shape.' Olu was to learn he had been there for eight days waiting for the ransom. He was sure that most people taken away never got to their families. He told Olu to eat as he may have a long wait. He did not think not eating was smart as these people thought out their strategies very carefully and they show no pity, so as smart as you may think you are, the graceful giraffe cannot become a monkey, he emphasized.

That night they came to the room and asked Olu and Chinedu and a few others for the numbers that they would call for ransom. Olu gazed unfocused but could remember his wife's name and Chinedu gave his brother number.

Olu had always told his wife what to do in a situation of this nature. As soon as she was called, she promised to empty the account which was jointly owned. First thing in the morning, she promised. Then she called her brother at Globacom and told him of the happenings. She gave the phone number they had used to call her and that at 8.o' clock she would be at the bank. But they used a different number to call her at 8.30, she told them there was eight million in the account; it was short of the ten million requested. They told her to keep her phone nearby. Chinedu's brother was asked to pay twenty million as business man. He negotiated to twelve million.

The same voice called Olu's wife the next day at 8am with instructions. She assured them everything was in order and sure that they would get good money from Olu and Chinedu Adamu informed the boss it was time to go collect. The boss never smiled and it was often difficult to tell when he was pleased but this time, Adamu could see from the gentle flash in his eyes, the news pleased him. Adamu took the opportunity to ask if they could keep Olu and let Chinedu go. Without looking at Adamu, he went back to the radio. With that refusal they went for the two men. The man next to him was asleep like most others in the room just as he had told Olu two nights earlier.

It was a pleasant surprise when Mustapha handed Olu's keys over to him and was asked to drive the car, his own car. Chinedu clasped his hands together behind him and said a silent prayer, '...for he will command His angels concerning you to guard you in all your ways.'

He knew Olu could handle these men, young and well-armed as they were. Adamu was intellectually sound but Olu was not only intellectually sound but well trained in the art of war. He hid all these behind a modest humility. Chinedu for the first time since their kidnap had some hope.

As they walked the little distance to where the cars were packed, the middle aged boss came out from behind a nearby hedge almost colliding with Adamu who stopped in his track. Without looking at the other three men, he handed Adamu an envelope with a stated amount on it. Adamu opened the envelope and took out a roll of foreign currency, counted and repeated the sum to his boss, 'seven thousand, five hundred dollars.'

'Send it to my son,' he said and turned to go.

'Which one?'

'Aminu,' then added as he walked away, 'dispose after the collection and give the car to Shatta Motors.'

They nodded even though the boss had disappeared in the direction he had come. They got into car after Olu had checked the water, oil and battery and with his foot, the baggage under the car. Chinedu made the sign of the cross, looked at Olu and could not hide a smile.

'What's funny,' Adamu asked getting into the car,

'Just thinking of my little daughter and how she would jump at me when she sees me,' he smiled widely, remembering his elders saying that when a goat laughs after hearing that a lion is around, one may need to find out what kind of grass it has been eating. Adamu was a little suspicious but with a rifle and a James Bond gun in his pocket and Adamu with a knife that would slice once through the neck, he hoped Chinedu would not be foolish. He preferred to keep Olu busy at the wheel because he could do more damage sitting.

Olu kicked the car hoping that Chinedu would realise that it is when we want to end pissing that it stains our pants. He turned onto the road he had not had an opportunity to go near since their arrival. Though he had been taken to some training grounds and made to install his inverter in one of the buildings, they made it clear that the out and inroad was out of bound and no one was ready to share with their teeth meat that they were not ready to eat.

This was their second trip on this road, now under the hot morning sun. Olu was sure if these people aimed to release them, they would have blindfolded them. What was the point in exposing them to this route and then release them to their families. Chinedu wondered who had built this road so far from human settlement. He wondered why people blamed the president. This was a military problem which only the military could tackle with its substantive budget. But then the president was a soldier who fought a civil war. There were rumours he was incapacitated by old age symptoms, and others with sinister intentions were running his government. There was more than meets the eye but as our elders rightly noted, Chinedu thought, the buttocks that remain for too long in the pit latrine will be visited by all kinds of flies. The president would do better to let his committed vice take over the government.

As Olu drove away his thoughts were on Maureen slowly being killed in the camp. The reflection of the hot sun on the bumper of the car ignited his anger as he remembered the young girl. She was on her way to her cousin's wedding in a bus to Kaduna when they were taken. While the boys in the bus were being trained as fighters, some girls were trained as bombers and others as wives and cooks. Among the trainers Olu had seen two Igbo young men who tried to hide their identity. One had later told Olu without looking at him that he should try and escape.

'They will not let you go after seeing this place.'

He had moved on and Olu could see a few eyes on them. He turned to a young man whom he engaged in conversation wondering aloud what an intelligent young man like him was doing there. He had told Olu he did not want to go back on the streets again. Why not go to school, Olu had asked.

He laughed.

'When I be small boy me and de boy chiren are told school not good. Years pass and we see our mate in de houses we work go school. Some we no see for long time, den dey come back and now now big man and spike Anglis. I late now to go school. Bet ma son will go to school not go to de street and I not allow ma young family member to be for road.'

Olu asked him if he thought it was government or the people he was helping in killing that were responsible for his situation. He said he did not know as a child but now he knew that he would not blame government. The schools were there for free. So it is not government. That is why he was advising all his siblings not to be like him, he emphasised, beating his chest. He said his siblings were all going to schools that he personally registered them in. For him the killings were to make a point...any point at all. He was looking after horses for a family whose children all went to school. He grew up with them. They did not care about him, yes! About you, he smiled. He said the children of the man who kept him as servant and told him school was not good for him were all in Abuja and him and his group were planning to visit him soon.

'We go see him in his house,' he said thumbing his chest as he walked away.

As Olu remembered that conversation, it dawned on him that most of the leaders of the insurgency were educated so why convince the young that it is forbidden? Or did they just wake up to that realisation? Olu wondered. The leader of this was sending money he had taken forcefully from others to send to his son schooling abroad. And not one son evident in the conversation between him and Adamu. Others around him were certainly not blind to his antics. Olu rubbed his thighs vigorously. He must not dwell on the damage done but focus on the now. He had his plan made to get away from these people and organize and come back for them and set free those in captivity.

They drove past a deserted village with a lost beauty of farms and no farmers to tend the crops. The land that stretched before and around the car cried out for tillage but no one to do so. A few crops of corn and millet, drop offs from a past when farmers had cropped the land, grew with the rains and then died off. Right now Olu just saw an expanse of wasted land with a long, empty, lonely road. He watched out for that felled electric or telephone pole he had marked out when they had stopped to urinate on their way to the forest. It should not be far away away, he was sure. He would tell the others he would ease himself. That was where Adamu and the others who knew the road had urinated on the herbs. Just then Mustapha interrupted his thoughts, 'I will empty myself,' he told Adamu.

Olu waited for him to get out before saying he too would do the same. Adamu nodded and came out of the car. Olu had been cooperative and useful in the previous day he had been under his watch especially at the training of young boys and girl bomber's with the creation of illusion of reality to illustrate behaviour at targeted venues. Olu never asked Adamu questions so as not to generate questions about himself. All he had told them was that he was a mechanic before he got a good job with a Foundation belonging to some Americans with good pay. He said he was on leave. What they didn't know was that Olu was in the mechanised unit of the Air force and on leave. He had a fake identity card which he carried on road trips. Too many colleagues had been killed on highways and it was foolish to pocket a uniformed ID. Many have been hacked to death for carrying uniforms in their cars.

Yesterday Adamu had tried to convince Bako the boss to keep Olu but Bako would not hear another word. He would not trust any smart man in the camp, not to mention outsiders like Olu. Adamu was trying to start a conversation by telling Olu he would have liked him to stay if the boss agreed. He would help with work on the training of recruits. He would not go for raids but he would be well paid, better than working for an NGO and he could send money to his family as most of them did. He was talking when they saw a black Hilux in the distance, the first vehicle since they were on the road. It had a problem. It had some of their camp's kidnappers at a deserted village where they had pushed the broken-down Hilux with a woman hostage. They had stopped to call the camp for another car when they saw Adamu who had asked Olu to check it. Olu fixed the car, but before they would leave told the woman to find a way of leaving the car in ten minutes, perhaps to vomit. The car would smoke and explode and until she got to a safe place, stay off the long, empty road. Cars on this road lead to the forest.

After fixing the car it was not long before Mustapha stopped to do the big one. He collected tissues from the box in the car. It was obvious this was a place they stopped for this. A few villages they passed, including the one with the broken-down Hilux ,were empty. Adamu said they avoided the villages because often the herdsmen occupied them and were not friendly. Around some villages were still dry sorghum, guinea corn, millet, signs that it had not been long humanity deserted those villages. Every now and again Olu had seen some herdsmen and their cattle, a few armed with AK47 rifles on their back. Olu hoped none would come along now as he was not sure what may happen. Mustapha had conveniently moved a distance into the bushy hedges. Olu stood outside the driver's door. Adamu did his exactly where Olu had hoped he would, by the back door where he had sat next to Chinedu. This gave Olu room to conveniently pee in a pure water bag, which he quickly emptied below the car, under the engine, then dropped the bag in the car where he would put his feet just as Mustapha walked to the driver's door. Olu pretended to lace his shoe which he had deliberately unlaced, 'I think there is a little leakage,' he said. He reached into the car and opened the bonnet.'

The two men bent and looked down and saw the wet ground and both walked to the front of the car. Chinedu remained in the car. Olu opened the door, took out the foot mat and threw it on the ground and lying on it, slid under the car. He unstrapped the phone, switched it on and sent his wife a message to call his second number. As he unstrapped the gun tied under the car, he heard the phone ring.

'Yes we are on our way. Have you got the money...go to the point I gave you and wait there... you want to talk to your...'

Olu shot him and put another shot into Mustapha's head as he bent to pick the gun. Chinedu pushed the door open and rushed to Olu. They picked the bodies and placed them behind the hedges, covered them with leaves, strapped one gun under the car and threw in the other one and placed the foot mat on it. Chinedu got into the car and drove it ahead while Olu covered up the evident signs of their presence on that spot. He hoped the bodies would not be found too soon.

As Olu got into the car he saw smoke in the distance and hoped the kidnapped woman had escaped. They had to get out of this road to the major road. It would be suicidal to go back to pick her as Bako the boss was likely to send a car to find out what had happened if the smoke was seen in the camp. And other cars may be on their way with people kidnapped.

They were quiet as their thoughts neither roamed distances that could not be controlled nor hearts that could not be tamed. They would have to return to Kano, and Olu would pick his wife and children to Lagos, stay quiet for a while and listen to the wind.

Chinedu drove through the once beautiful, peaceful country with children running around the farms at harvest time. He wanted to believe that peace would be back again and the houses would ring with laughter. He wanted to believe this was a passing phase.

'Call my brother,' he told Olu.

He thought of the dying girl and the man and his wife. The woman with the Hilux had to find her way. She had a long way to go on the long and empty road.

Printed in the United States
By Bookmasters